Helping Children Learn

Helping Children Learn

Intervention Handouts for Use in School and at Home

by

Jack A. Naglieri, Ph.D.
George Mason University
Fairfax, Virginia

and

Eric B. Pickering, Ph.D.
Grandview Heights City Schools
Grandview, Ohio

·P A U L·H·
BROOKES
PUBLISHING Co®

Baltimore • London • Sydney

Paul H. Brookes Publishing Co.
Post Office Box 10624
Baltimore, Maryland 21285-0624

www.brookespublishing.com

Typeset by Barton Matheson Willse & Worthington, Baltimore, Maryland.
Manufactured in the United States of America by
Versa Press, Inc., East Peoria, Illinois.

All case studies in this book are based on the authors' actual experiences. In all instances, names have been changed; in some instances, identifying details have been altered to further protect confidentiality.

Case study illustrations by Dirk Rozich.

Library of Congress Cataloging-in-Publication Data

Naglieri, Jack A.
  Helping children learn : intervention handouts for use in school and at home / by Jack A.
  Naglieri and Eric B. Pickering.
    p.   cm.
  Includes bibliographical references and index.
  ISBN 1-55766-646-6
  1. Learning disabled children—Education.   2. Academic achievement.   3. Cognition in
  children—Testing.   I. Pickering, Eric B.   II. Title.

  LC4704.5.N34   2003
  371.92'6—dc21   2003043794

British Library Cataloguing in Publication data are available from the British Library.

Contents

About the Authors

Jack A. Naglieri, Ph.D., is Professor of Psychology and Director of the Center for Cognitive Development at George Mason University in Fairfax, Virginia. He has written more than 150 publications including scientific journal articles, book chapters, books, tests, and computer software programs. For his scholarly efforts, Dr. Naglieri was awarded the American Psychological Association's 2001 Senior Scientist Award. He has devoted most of his career to the study of intelligence and its relationship to learning and learning problems.

Eric B. Pickering, Ph.D., is School Psychologist at the Grandview Heights City Schools in Grandview, Ohio. He has considerable experience with working in all levels of schools and especially with applying the interventions included in this book. Dr. Pickering has focused his efforts on the development of practical methods for teachers and school psychologists because of his desire to give educational professionals well-researched instructional interventions that can help children learn.

Preface

This book provides brief summaries of ways in which teachers and parents can help children learn academic and related skills. The interventions were selected because they can help children learn a variety of academic skills and because they can be related to how children think. When these interventions are paired with knowledge about a child's cognitive weaknesses and strengths, teachers and parents may be better able to help the child learn. For this reason, we have combined a way of thinking about children's abilities with methods of teaching.

The book has two parts. Part I includes Chapters 1–3, which describe the concepts associated with education that take into consideration how children think, and outlines how to use the handouts to help children learn. Part II presents the interventions as convenient handouts that can be easily shared among parents, teachers, and other professionals, such as the school psychologist. These handouts are provided as a resource for psychologists who work with educational issues. We anticipate that these professionals will have information about how the child learns that is relevant to the selection of these handouts (see Chapter 2). The handouts may be useful for teachers and parents trying to help children who have specific academic problems.

Index of Handouts

	Handout	Planning	Attention	Simultaneous processing	Successive processing
PASS	Planning Explained (pp. 37–38)	●			
	Attention Explained (pp. 39–40)		●		
	Simultaneous Processing Explained (pp. 41–42)			●	
	Successive Processing Explained (pp. 43–44)				●
General	Overcoming Problems with Inattention (pp. 45–46)	●			
	Plans for Remembering (pp. 47–48)		●		
	Self-Monitoring for Planning and Attention Problems (pp. 49–50)	●	●		
	Graphic Organizers for Connecting and Remembering Information (pp. 51–52)			●	
	Stop and Think! Teaching Self-Control (pp. 53–54)	●			
	Teaching Self-Awareness (pp. 55–56)	●			
	Promoting Good Listening (p. 57)		●		
	Teaching Good Thinking Skills (pp. 59–60)	●			
	Strategies for Improving Organization (pp. 61–62)	●		●	
	Improving Attention (pp. 63–64)		●		
	Making a Plan for Organizing (p. 65)	●			
Reading	Summarization Strategy for Reading Comprehension (pp. 67–68)			●	
	Plans for Understanding Text (pp. 69–70)	●			
	Plans for Reading Comprehension (pp. 71–72)	●			
	Chunking for Reading/Decoding (p. 73)				●
	Word Families for Reading/Decoding (pp. 75–76)			●	
	Story Grammar for Reading Comprehension (pp. 77–78)				●
	Reading/Decoding Rules (pp. 79–80)				●
	Segmenting Words for Reading/Decoding and Spelling (p. 81)				●
	Letter–Sound Awareness (pp. 83–84)				●
	Plans for Word Syllables (p. 85)				●

	Handout	Planning	Attention	Simultaneous processing	Successive processing
Spelling	Word Sorts for Improving Spelling (p. 87)			●	
	Chunking for Spelling (p. 89)				●
	Letter Ordering for Spelling (pp. 91–92)				●
	Mnemonics for Spelling (pp. 93–94)	●			
	Strategies for Spelling (pp. 95–96)	●			●
Writing	Story Plans for Written Composition (pp. 97–98)				
	Plans for Writing (pp. 99–100)	●			
	Story Grammar for Writing (p. 101)				●
	Teaching Vocabulary Using Visual Cues (p. 103)			●	
	Planning by Writing Sentence Openers (pp. 105–106)	●		●	
	Planning to Write (p. 107)	●			
Math	Planning Facilitation for Math Calculation (pp. 109–110)	●			
	Number Squares for Math Concepts (pp. 111–112)				●
	Plans for Basic Math Facts (pp. 113–114)	●			
	Cuisenaire Rods and Math (pp. 115–116)			●	
	TouchMath for Calculation (pp. 117–118)				●
	Part–Whole Strategy for Math Calculation (pp. 119–120)	●			●
	Seven-Step Strategy for Math Word Problems (pp. 121–122)	●	●	●	●
	Chunking Strategy for Multiplication (pp. 123–124)				●
	Crossed Lines Multiplication Strategy (p. 125)			●	
	More Strategies for Math Word Problems (pp. 127–128)	●	●	●	●
Test taking	General Strategies for Test Taking (p. 129)	●			
	Strategies for Multiple Choice, Matching, and True–False Tests (p. 131)	●			
	Strategies for Written Tests (p. 133)	●			

Acknowledgments

We extend our sincere thanks to all those who gave us feedback and support during the various stages of development of this book. We thank the teachers and parents of the Grandview Heights City Schools and the many professionals who attended workshops on assessments that lead to intervention for serving as a testing ground for the handouts. We also thank people at Paul H. Brookes Publishing Co. We give a special thanks to Dr. Sam Goldstein for the excellent feedback he gave on an earlier version of the handouts included in this book. We thank the school psychology graduate students for their thoughtful comments on the PASS Rating Scale. We also thank Sara Temple for her thoughtful review of the handouts and her trusty companion Jasper Temple for his patience. Finally, we thank Diane, Andrea, Antonia, and Jack Jr. for their continued support and tolerance of the long hours we spent at home and in the office working on the book.

Helping others was one of the most significant lessons I learned from my parents as a young person. Through their many kind and selfless efforts, they taught me that being helpful to someone is a noble act that can have profound impact. This book is the unanticipated result of the example my parents gave of the importance of helping others. For this reason, I dedicate my efforts on this book to my mother, Martha Naglieri, and my father, Sam Naglieri (1926–2001). Thank you, Mom and Dad, for the extraordinary example you gave me.—JAN

I recognize the skill, patience, and dedication of the many teachers and parents who meet the everyday challenge of helping children succeed with whom I have worked. It is to these people who work so hard to make the lives of our children, and thus all our lives, better that I dedicate this work. Specifically, I'd like to dedicate my efforts to many of the special education staff and staff in the Grandview Heights City Schools including Naomi Allison, Cristy Graves, Lindsay Graves, Diane Mountz, Megan Rowles, Diane Runyon, and Judy Sargeant.—EBP

Part I

Introduction

Chapter 1

Using This Book

This book provides practical methods for teachers and parents to use to help children acquire academic knowledge and skills. The practical methods provided in this book are short instructional interventions that are designed to cover specific academic areas (e.g., reading/decoding) or topics (e.g., test taking). Educational professionals can give the handouts to educators and parents who are working to help children learn. The methods can be applied on the basis of the academic area of need (e.g., difficulties with reading, spelling, or math calculation), or they can be used in conjunction with information provided by the school psychologist or a similar professional about the child's intellectual strengths and weaknesses.

The interventions presented in this book were identified among a variety of resources and included if there was empirical support for the approach. In addition, these particular interventions were selected because they are consistent with our understanding of the ways in which children think. Understanding how a child thinks, especially if the child has an academic difficulty, can help determine which particular handouts to use to improve learning. For example, there can be many reasons why a child has difficulty with comprehending what he or she has read. The child may have problems reading individual words, concentrating, following the sequence of the events, or seeing the big picture. If the child has problems with seeing the story as a whole (i.e., seeing how things are connected), this may lead the school professional to select an intervention that makes connections more obvious. Later in this chapter, a description of this type of an intervention and ways to select the interventions are included. First, it is important to recognize a few things about how children learn.

Learning has been described as a complicated event in which the teacher, the setting, the curriculum, the family structure, the way a child thinks, and many other factors all lead to academic success or failure (Naglieri & Ashman, 1999). Educators and parents often spend a considerable amount of time managing all of these factors that influence learning, especially when children begin to experience academic problems. When a child is experiencing problems, school professionals, educators, and parents often look for alternative ways to teach—that is what these handouts provide. The instructional handouts are intended to provide methods or techniques that a teacher or parent can use to help a child learn better. These handouts can be used very effectively when the factors associated with a child's academic problem are known.

Knowing what factors are related to a child's academic problems can help educators and parents be more effective. Sometimes a child experiences academic failure because of inconsistent knowledge and skills. In these cases, careful analysis of what the child knows can be very helpful. Sometimes the classroom has to be modified to help the child learn better. Other times knowing about a child's characteristics can be informative. For example, the child may have some sensory difficulty, an emotional or behavioral problem, or variation in his or her abilities that interferes with learning. When a child's intellectual strengths and weaknesses play an important role in academic performance, the interventions in this book should be carefully selected. Instructional methods in this book can be efficiently applied when a child's *intellectual strengths and weaknesses,* as well as academic strengths and weaknesses, are known (Naglieri & Ashman, 1999; Peverly, 1994).

The remainder of this book describes cognitive strengths and weaknesses and children's cognitive processing levels. The term *cognitive processing* is used instead of the term *intelligence* because it is a more modern and useful way of thinking about children's abilities. We use the term *cognitive processes* to talk about specific types of abilities more fully described later in this chapter. These abilities are more strongly related to children's academic success and failure than what is typically described as intelligence (Naglieri, 1999). This cognitive processing perspective also helps school professionals, educators, and parents to better understand why some children have problems with learning and to match a child's cognitive processing strengths and weaknesses with specific ways of teaching (see Part II of this book) (Naglieri & Johnson, 2000).

The PASS cognitive processing weaknesses described in this book can also be used to help determine whether a child has a learning disability (LD). Federal and state definitions of LD typically describe it as a disorder in one or more basic psychological processes involved in understanding or using language that manifests itself in an imperfect ability to listen, think, speak, read, write, spell, or do mathematical calculations. This means that if a child has a PASS cognitive weakness and academic failure like the children described in this book, then the child's PASS weakness (in combination with other data) may be used to support the diagnosis of LD. Knowing that a child has a cognitive processing weakness can also help educators teach that child more effectively.

Children's cognitive processes are relevant to learning because they influence how a child approaches tasks and how successful a child can be. The connection between cognitive processing and achievement is well documented (Naglieri & Das, 1997a, 1997b; Naglieri & Rojahn, 2002). These authors have found that tests of cognitive processing, such as the Kaufman Assessment Battery for Children (Kaufman

& Kaufman, 1983) and the Cognitive Assessment System (CAS; Naglieri & Das, 1997a), measure the ways children think that are strongly related to achievement in a variety of areas. Cognitive processes are relevant to learning and, therefore, to instruction.

The strong relationship between cognitive processing and learning suggests that if school psychologists, educators, and parents know the child's strengths and weaknesses, they can do a more efficient job of teaching the child. This is where teamwork comes into play. The school psychologist knows how to determine a child's cognitive processing strengths and weaknesses. The teacher has much instructional experience with the child. The parents know their child and can help create a good system of instructional support for the child at home. Working together, the school psychologist can provide important information about the child's cognitive strengths and weaknesses and, along with the teacher and parents, identify instructional methods that best fit the child. The instructional methods presented in this book are designed to facilitate this interaction based on good cognitive processing principles that the educator or parent can easily use. These handouts can also be used in a variety of ways to help children learn, which are more fully described in the next chapter.

HOW TO USE THE INTERVENTIONS

Part II of this book contains many handouts. Some are information sheets, some discuss skill-building, and others describe specific activities. The handouts can be applied in at least two ways, which are illustrated in Figure 1.1. This flow chart begins with Box 1, the belief that a child has an academic problem in a specific skill area about which the teacher or parent has concerns. For example, a child may have problems with reading individual words. The first step, Box 2, is to select a handout based on the academic area. This can be accomplished by referring to the index organized by academic area on page 34 of this book. Next, the intervention should be applied and progress monitored (Box 3). Following the use of the instructional method, the question in Box 4 should be asked, "Did the intervention work?" If so, then efforts to cope with the problem are completed (Box 5). If the result of the intervention was not satisfactory, then it becomes important to know whether there is some other reason why the child's response was limited. At this point, it can be useful to involve a school psychologist or a similar professional to find out if the child has some type of cognitive processing weakness that may be interfering with learning (Box 6).

If this is the first time an intervention has been tried (Box 7), and it is found that the child does have a cognitive processing weakness, then it is important to select the handouts in Section II with consideration of that weakness (Box 8). These interventions should be applied and evaluated (back to Box 3). If they have limited effectiveness, then the child's academic problem requires more intensive intervention methods and an even closer examination of the various reasons for the learning problem (Box 9).

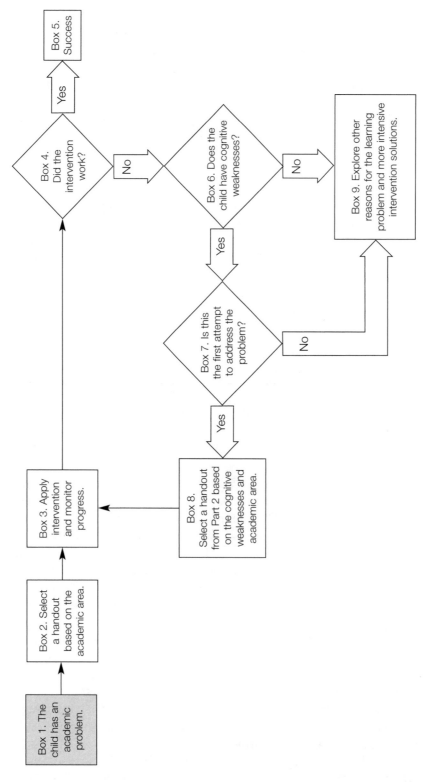

Figure 1.1. The process of using the handouts in Part II.

CONCLUSION

The instructional handouts presented in this book provide practical methods that can be used by teachers and parents to help children acquire knowledge and skills. This chapter outlines how the instructional handouts could be used when a child has a specific academic need. It also shows how academic interventions can be applied when there is a cognitive processing strength or weakness that is related to the learning problem. This type of teaching requires an examination of the tasks with which a child is having problems from both an academic skill requirement perspective and a cognitive processing perspective. When both of these dimensions are taken into consideration, effective teaching and learning can result.

Chapter 2

Cognitive Processes

Chapter 1 introduced concepts about children's strengths and weaknesses in cognitive processes and used this description as a modern way to talk about ability. In this book, we refer to a theory called PASS, which stands for *P*lanning, *A*ttention, *Si*multaneous, and *S*uccessive cognitive processes (Naglieri, 1999). The PASS cognitive processes are ways in which people think, learn, and solve problems. These processes are involved in reading, writing, and doing math, as well as everyday activities such as driving a car or cooking a dinner. PASS processes underlie the acquisition of knowledge and skills (along with other important variables such as motivation, family attitudes toward school, completion of homework, and so forth). The four types of processes have specific definitions that are described in the sections that follow.

PASS

The four PASS processes are concepts that are used to describe how people think, learn, and solve problems. PASS processes are similar to the concepts of ability, aptitude, or intelligence because they provide information about how "smart" a child is. This theory describes four types of abilities, but we prefer to think about them as basic psychological processes. The choice of these particular cognitive processes is based on research about the brain and how it works, in particular, the Russian neuropsychologist A.R. Luria's views (1966, 1973, 1980) about how the human brain processes information.

Research findings about how the brain works and the cognitive processes involved can help school psychologists, teachers, and parents better understand a child's abilities and his or her cognitive processing strengths or weaknesses. This information can also help adults understand why the child may be good or weak in some academic areas. This information can then be used to select ways of teaching the child. For example, if the teacher knows that a child is weak in a particular type of cognitive processing, he or she should avoid using an instruction method that relies considerably on that type of thinking.

In order for a child to complete an academic task such as math calculation, for example, many factors are involved. First, the child has to be interested, willing, alert, focused, and emotionally ready to perform the task. Second, the child needs to have the basic skills (i.e., knowledge) relevant to the problem (e.g., knowledge of math facts). Third, the child needs to have the ability to think in order to solve the problem. What type of thinking is needed depends on the demands of the task. Some tasks require a considerable amount of planning and strategizing in order to arrive at the correct answer. Other parts of the task may require careful attention to the details, and still others may involve understanding the sequence of events or how various parts of the problem are related. Cognitive processes are needed for learning, and knowledge is important for the use of processes. Because processes are important when a child applies his or her knowledge and skills, it is important to know when a child has a cognitive strength or weakness. When teachers and parents understand that a child's poor academic performance may be related to a cognitive processing problem, then they can better select instructional methods. But first a better understanding of the psychological processes, the different ways of thinking, and how they relate to learning is needed.

Planning

The first cognitive process is called *planning*. Planning is a way of thinking that a person uses to evaluate a task, select or develop a way of doing something (i.e., a strategy to approach a task), monitor progress, and develop new strategies when necessary. This process provides control of thought as well as the use of other processes, knowledge, and skills. For example, when a child is faced with a task that demands that he or she figure out a way to do it, then planning is involved. Sometimes the way children are taught can involve planning.

The spelling study guide shown in Figure 2.1 is a way of teaching that encourages students to consider different ways to learn weekly spelling words. The instructional sheet does

This Week's Spelling Words

Here are the words for this Friday's test:

1. found
2. ground
3. mouth
4. ouch
5. couch
6. count
7. round
8. out
9. shout
10. north
11. south
12. east
13. west
14. globe
15. robe

How will you learn the words?

1. Start today
2. Study 15 minutes per day
3. Study with a friend
4. Write each word 10 times
5. Make flashcards
6. Make a word search puzzle

What other ways to learn these words can you think of? Write them down!

_____

_____

_____

_____

Figure 2.1. A classroom exercise that requires planning processing.

not simply tell the child what words to learn but instead encourages children to choose an activity that will help them learn the words. These methods (e.g., study with a friend, make flashcards) encourage children to think about how to learn. Because this worksheet puts the emphasis on strategies for how to learn to spell, it involves planning. Children who make good plans have lots of ways of doing things and are effective at coming up with strategies. Children who cannot plan well struggle with how to do things. They may use the same strategy even if it is not very effective, and they are often disorganized.

Attention

Attention is a way of thinking that allows a child to focus on one thing and ignore others. Resisting distractions in the environment is an important part of attention. In the classroom, this process allows a child to selectively focus on things heard or seen (e.g., the teacher) and resist being distracted by less relevant sights and sounds (e.g., children talking outside the room). Another illustration is provided in Figure 2.2. In this example, the child must focus on the specific question and examine the options carefully while at the same time ignoring the answers that are wrong but may be very close to the correct answer. For example, in the math problem "What is the number for 5 tens and 2 ones?" the child must pick from several similar answers. Because these options are so similar, there are many distractions. This makes it hard for the child to determine which option is the correct one. The "respond" or "do not respond" situation demands considerable attention. Children who score high in attention processing can concentrate well and resist distractions. Those who score low have trouble focusing on what is important, working on the same task for very long, concentrating on one topic, and seeing all of the details.

Simultaneous Processing

The third process is *simultaneous* processing, which a child uses to relate separate pieces of information into a group or to see how parts are related as a whole. Simultaneous processing is also used when a child has to recognize patterns. For this reason, simultaneous processing is important for doing geometry, seeing patterns in numbers, seeing a group of letters as a word, seeing words as a whole, understanding a sentence as part of a

---

Math Worksheet for Tens and Ones

Name: _____   Date: _____

Circle the correct answers.

1. What is the number for 5 tens and 2 ones?

    50   25   52   502   55

2. Which number has a 2 in the tens place and a 7 in the ones place?

    27   270   72   22   702

3. Which number has a 5 in the tens place and a 4 in the ones place?

    504   54   55   45   50

4. Which number has a 6 in the tens place and a 9 in the ones place?

    66   690   96   69   996

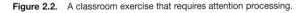

Figure 2.2.   A classroom exercise that requires attention processing.

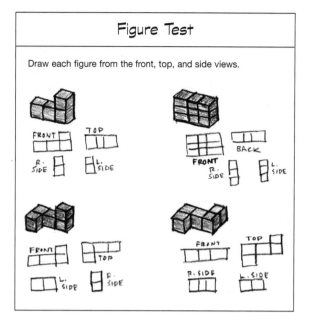

Figure 2.3. A classroom exercise that requires simultaneous processing.

paragraph, and seeing how a paragraph fits as part of a complete story. Simultaneous processing is involved in reading comprehension because it requires the integration and understanding of word relationships and how all of the elements of a text fit together. Figure 2.3 provides a good example of a geometry problem that requires simultaneous processing. In this example, the child has to draw the diagram from each of the four perspectives. Seeing how an image should look from the various perspectives involves simultaneous processing. Children who are good at simultaneous processing easily understand how pieces of a whole fit together. Children who score low in this process do not understand how things are related, have trouble with spatial relationships, and often miss the overall idea.

Successive Processing

The fourth process is *successive* processing, which is what a child uses to work with information that is arranged in order. Whenever information must be organized or kept in specific order so that the parts are correctly sequenced, successive processing is involved. Successive processing is also important whenever comprehension is based on appreciation of the order of events. For instance, successive processing is involved in remembering a series of words or numbers and blending sounds to form words because the child has to do things in a specific order. Figure 2.4 provides an

Words with Similar Sounds

Name: _____ Date: _____

Copy each sentence carefully.

1. Arty ate apples.

_____

2. Larry lost his little lock.

_____

3. She sees sea shells by the sea.

_____

4. Betty bought a box of baseballs.

_____

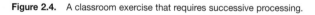

Figure 2.4. A classroom exercise that requires successive processing.

example of tasks that involve considerable sequencing of words (saying the short sentences), sounds (articulating the sounds of the words to say them properly), and letters (writing the words using the correct sequence of letters). In this example, the similarity of the words makes this particularly difficult. Children who have strong successive processing are able to remember things in order, work with information that is linearly organized, and follow instructions that are presented in sequence. Children who have weak successive processing struggle to arrange information in a specific sequence, understand information presented in sequence, or remember information in a series.

MEASURING PASS PROCESSES

The four PASS processes can be thought of as four separate abilities that children have that are related to how well they learn. These processes have to be measured to provide information about how well a child uses these important processes. Although school psychologists, teachers, and parents can sometimes get an idea about how well a child can use the PASS processes by observation (see the rating scale presented later in this chapter), the best way to measure these processes is to assess the child using an individually administered test.

The CAS (Naglieri & Das, 1997a) was developed specifically to measure the PASS cognitive processes. The individually administered test provides a window into the way children think, learn, and solve problems using the four PASS processes. This test is administered and interpreted by a specially trained professional, such as a school psychologist. Because the teachers and parents who use this book are also consumers of the information about PASS, we have provided several pieces of information about the PASS processes on the test and handouts for their use (see Part II).

The CAS gives four scores, one for each PASS process, that can be used to describe a child's cognitive processing strengths and weaknesses. The scale is set so that a score of 100 is average, a score of 115 is above average, and a score of 89 is below average. A score of 89 means that the child only did as well as or better than 16% of children who are his or her age. A child with a score of 89 or less has considerable difficulty with solving problems using that type of cognitive process. A score of 115 means that the child is doing as well as or better than 84% of children his or her age. For all these PASS scores, an average score (100) means that the child did as well as or better than 50% of children.

All of the PASS scores are organized into a classification system shown in Table 2.1 for easier interpretation. This table, which comes from the *CAS Interpretive Handbook* (Naglieri & Das,

Table 2.1. Classification of Cognitive Assessment System (CAS) full scale and PASS scale scores

Score	Ability
130 and above	Very superior
120–129	Superior
110–119	High average
90–109	Average
80–89	Low average
70–79	Below average
69 and below	Well below average

1997b), describes the scores a child can earn on the PASS scales of the CAS and provides a useful way to describe or classify them.

The scores on the separate PASS Scales represent a child's cognitive functioning in the four distinct areas of cognitive processing or ability, and they are used to identify specific strengths and weaknesses. When a child has very different scores on these four scales, the information can be used to identify specific cognitive processing weaknesses or strengths. In general, if a child has one or two PASS scores that are below 85 and the other PASS scores are average or above, this may be evidence of a cognitive processing weakness. The determination of a cognitive processing weakness should be made by a school psychologist or other similarly trained professional.

The procedures for determining whether a child has a PASS weakness or strength are found in the book *Essentials of CAS Assessment* (Naglieri, 1999). The methods described there allow a school psychologist, or a similarly trained professional, to determine when one (or more) score is low enough to be considered a weakness or high enough to be considered a strength. This information can be used to guide the selection of the handouts. For example, if the child is trying to learn basic math facts and is being asked to repeat the facts in order (e.g., $7 + 8 = 15$), then the task of memorization requires much successive processing (Kroesbergen, van Luit, & Naglieri, in press). Children who score low in successive processing are likely to have difficulty remembering the sum of $7 + 8$ because they may not be able to remember more than three things in order. If it is known that the child has a weakness in successive processing (but has average scores in the other PASS processes), then a strategy that involves planning can be used to help the child remember more efficiently. For example, the child may be taught the "doubles plus one" rule (see page 113). This instructional approach reduces the successive processing demands of the task.

SIGNS OF PROCESSING PROBLEMS IN THE CLASSROOM

Educators and parents may be able to observe a child's behaviors and find some indication of the child's competence with the PASS processes. An observant teacher or parent can detect clues that suggest how well the child uses the PASS processes. This observational approach has value—especially if combined with information from the CAS—when using these handouts to help children learn better. Although it is possible to see signs that suggest if a child has strong or weak ability in each of the four processes, ultimately a thorough and accurate examination of the child's processes is best obtained by administering the CAS.

Educators and parents can get an idea of how competent a child is in PASS processes by completing the informal rating scale provided in Figure 2.5. To use this rating scale, the teacher or parent answers the questions on the scale, "Always," "Usually," "Sometimes," or "Never." After all of the questions have been answered, the teacher or parent should examine the scores within each PASS area (the items are in four groups designated by bold horizontal lines). The items are grouped in the planning, simultaneous, attention, successive order that corresponds to the order in

PASS Rating Scale (PRS)

Child's name: _____   Person completing the form: _____

Test date: _____   Relationship to the child: _____

Directions: This scale contains descriptions of behaviors that can help determine how well the child can use important cognitive processes. To use this scale, rate the questions on the basis of your knowledge of the child. Read each statement and put a checkmark under the word that tells how often you observed the behavior. If you want to change your answer, cross out your first response and fill in your new choice. Answer every question.

During the past 2 months, how often did the child	Always	Usually	Sometimes	Never
1. Work in a well-organized and neat way				
2. Use strategies and plans when doing work				
3. Evaluate his or her own behavior				
4. Think before acting				
5. Have many ideas about how to do things				
6. Show self-control				
7. Perform well on spatial activities (e.g., maps, diagrams)				
8. Understand how things go together				
9. See the big picture				
10. Understand complex verbal instructions				
11. Work well with patterns				
12. Like to use visual materials				
13. Focus well on one thing				
14. Work without being distracted by people or noises				
15. Pay close attention				
16. Listen to instructions without being distracted				
17. Work well for a long time				
18. Work well in a noisy environment				
19. Work well with information in sequence				
20. Do well with things presented step by step				
21. Remember the order of information				
22. Understand directions presented in sequence				
23. Do well working with sounds in order				
24. Closely follow directions presented in order				

Figure 2.5. The PASS rating scale. Copyright © 1997 by The Riverside Publishing Company. All rights reserved. Reproduced from the "Das Naglieri Cognitive Assessment System" by Jack Naglieri and J.P. Das. No part of this work may be reproduced or transmitted in any form or by any means, electronic or mechanical, including photocopying and recording, or by any information storage or retrieval system without the prior written permission of The Riverside Publishing Company unless such copying is expressly permitted by federal copyright law. Address inquiries to Permissions, The Riverside Publishing Company, 425 Spring Lake Drive, Itasca, Illinois 60143-2079.

Table 2.2. Signs of learning problems and associated PASS processes

Planning	Problems developing strategies to read or spell words Failure to correct misinterpretation of a sentence Inconsistent spelling of words and repetition of errors Random attempts to solve math problems Lack of strategies for solving problems Failure to switch math or reading strategies when necessary
Attention	Short attention span in a variety of activities Failure to resist distractions in the environment Slow recall of basic facts Failure to attend to new information Failure to notice details Failure to attend to one thing when required to do so
Simultaneous processing	Failure to recognize sight words or use word shapes for cues Failure to interpret word, sentence, or paragraph meaning Failure to see syllables in words Failure to see groups of letters when spelling words Failure to comprehend text, especially in math word problems Unfamiliarity of math concepts, patterns, and problem types
Successive processing	Poor word analysis skills and inability to sound out words Lack of comprehension based on word order Failure to pronounce words correctly Failure to retain place (loss of sound segments) in word being spelled Loss of place in sequence when counting or doing math problems Failure to follow word, sentence, or paragraph sequence when reading

Source: Kirby and Williams (1991).

which the CAS scales are sequenced. For those PASS areas that are typically rated "Always" and "Usually," it can be assumed that the child is competent. Conversely, when the child's ratings are usually "Sometimes" or "Never," this suggests that the child may be weak in that particular process.

Teachers and parents can also get an indication of the child's ability to use the PASS processes by careful observation of his or her behavior in class and at home. In order to connect some of these observations with the PASS cognitive processes, we have summarized information from a section of the book *Learning Problems: A Cognitive Approach* (Kirby & Williams, 1991) in Table 2.2. This table gives some examples; others can be obtained directly from the Kirby and Williams book.

CONCLUSION

In this chapter, we define children's abilities using the PASS theory of cognitive processing. We look at the four PASS processes, how they relate to academic achievement, and how these abilities can be measured. In addition to the formal method of testing the PASS processes using the CAS, an informal PASS Rating Scale is provided. This scale allows teachers and parents to estimate a child's ability to use the four PASS cognitive processes. Finally, a discussion of academic signs of PASS processes in the classroom or at home is provided.

Chapter 3

Case Illustrations

This chapter explains how the handouts were used with children we have encountered in our practice. Each child had problems at school that seriously affected his or her success, and the teacher or parents requested assistance from one of us. Rather than present complete psychoeducational reports for each of these children, we selected the most relevant information to provide for illustration purposes. Each case includes facts about the academic problem the student was experiencing and what the parents and teachers said about the child. Although the examples here are real students, their names and identifying features have been changed to protect their privacy.

Our analysis of each of the cases in this chapter progressed in a specific sequence illustrated in Figure 1.1. We began by assessing the situation, paying careful attention to all dimensions of the academic problem, and trying to determine if there was some straightforward solution. Our initial informal evaluation centered on the teacher's observations of the learning problem. For example, if a teacher or parent noted that a student had particular difficulty writing a story (Box 1) and that the child seemed to have trouble planning how to write the story, selection of an appropriate handout (Box 2) could be made on the basis of the academic problem. At this point, the selected intervention would be applied (Box 3) and if it was effective (Box 4), then the issue would be solved (Box 5). In this book, we only illustrate those cases in which it was necessary to go beyond this point. When the intervention did not appear to work or its effectiveness was limited, it may have been because the child had a cognitive processing weakness (Box 6).

When this stage is reached in an intervention, teachers and parents usually work in collaboration with educational specialists such as school psychologists to obtain more information about how the child learns and in particular, the child's

PASS processing levels. It may become apparent that there is a cognitive weakness related to the learning problem, and a handout should be selected which takes that weakness into consideration (Box 8). (If this is not the first time the child has gone through the process, teachers and parents should explore other reasons for the learning problem and more intensive intervention solutions, as in Box 9.) For example, when a child has an academic problem and is weak in some area of cognitive processing, the cognitive demands of the academic task should be carefully examined. Interventions that help the child use a different process when doing the particular academic task should then be considered. That is, it may be helpful to use a different instructional approach that has a different cognitive processing demand.

At this point in the procedure, the selection of handouts from this book should be made with consideration of the cognitive demands of that academic task (Box 8). The concept is that when a child has a cognitive weakness, that specific weakness may be incompatible with the way instruction was presented. The child is more likely to be successful when an instructional handout is selected that does not rely so heavily on the process with which the child has problems. Shifting the cognitive processing demand of a task is an excellent intervention because it helps the child perform a task in a way that does not rely on his or her cognitive weakness. It also gives the child a chance to be successful.

To achieve the goal of selecting methods that address the processing demands of a task, it is important to carefully examine the extent to which the PASS processes are involved in the academic task. For example, a child may have trouble with reading/decoding because he or she cannot sequence the sounds of the words effectively. The child who struggles with successive processing is likely to have problems working with information in a specific series (e.g., sounds of words in order). That is, the task involves successive processing and the child is poor in that cognitive process. The goal would be to find a method of teaching reading/decoding that does not place so much emphasis on successive processing (because the child is weak in that process). The Chunking for Reading/Decoding handout (p. 73) teaches the child to use a strategy for reading/decoding rather than trying to sound out the word. When a strategy or plan is used in this way, the child can find the correct answer by thinking about the problem (planning or being strategic) rather than by trying to decode the word in segments (which demands much successive processing). This change in the instruction changes the cognitive demands of the task.

Another way to help the student is to teach him or her specific strategies or plans to complete academic tasks (Naglieri & Gottling, 1997; Naglieri & Johnson, 2000). For example, a student who struggles with planning may have trouble writing stories or reports because he or she does not have a good way of approaching the task. Using the handout Planning by Writing Sentence Openers (p. 105) gives this type of student a way to plan out the story or report. This helps the child overcome his or her weakness in generating a plan. It can also help the student learn how to solve problems and become an effective learner.

Once the interventions are applied (Box 3 in Figure 1.1) with consideration of the relationship between the child's academic needs and cognitive processing weakness, then the question in Box 4 is asked again: "Did the intervention work?" If so, then the difficulty is addressed; if not, then further problem solving is required to

18

address the child's learning problem. This is likely to involve exploration of other reasons for the learning problem and more intensive and complex interventions. The case studies that follow provide examples of instances in which the intervention handouts were effective.

CHRISTINE'S TROUBLE WITH PLANNING

Christine was a pleasant sixth-grade student who seemed a little shy and anxious but responded well in one-to-one interactions. She had an excellent attendance record but was occasionally late for school and back to class after lunch. Christine usually sat at the side of the classroom and did not interact very much with the other students. She typically did not raise her hand to answer questions but occasionally blurted out the answer. Sometimes in class, Christine did not appear engaged in an activity. Some of the more troublesome problems her teachers reported were that she often did not pay attention, finish her work on time, or do what was instructed.

At the beginning of the school year, Christine and her classmates were given a long-term assignment that involved collecting newspaper articles about a topic and then creating a poster and writing a report. The day the project was assigned, Christine worked with other students to go through newspapers and brainstorm ideas. She had trouble picking a topic and repeatedly asked her fellow students and the teacher the purpose of the project. She finally arrived at a topic after considerable effort. Throughout the following month, students periodically had opportunities to work on the project in class. Christine usually appeared unprepared and disorganized, and it was apparent that she did not make much progress. Her teachers offered some help but felt it was her responsibility to complete the project on time. The day before the project was due, Christine became panicked when she realized that she was not prepared. She appeared as if she did not quite know what to do. Christine did not, however, ask for help or look at her classmate's projects for ideas. That night Christine's mother called the teacher, and she reported she did not know about the project and needed information so she could help Christine. The next day, Christine came to school late but did have the project finished. The project's quality was minimally acceptable, and the teacher discovered upon further inspection that Christine worked on it only twice during the 1-month time period.

Christine's parents expressed exasperation at her frequent failure to finish homework, keep organized, and successfully plan out projects. They noted that she had constant trouble getting started and seemed not to know what to do or how to structure her academic and personal activities. They also complained that Christine constantly needs to be prompted to do basic daily tasks like finishing work, getting ready for school, getting ready for bed, and even for getting ready for activities she was excited about. Christine's parents had considered consulting a professional regarding attention-deficit/hyperactivity disorder, but they noted that Christine can concentrate well and pay attention when she puts her mind to it. They found that at home, she can spend hours doing artwork, talking to her sister, or working alongside her mother without seeming inattentive or distracted.

Christine's grades were poorest in science class, where she was assigned a lot of long-term projects, and in English class, where she had to do a lot of writing. She also performed poorly in math class, particularly on homework and word problems. In science, she often did not finish projects or left out important parts of the assignment. In English, she typically took a long time to pick a topic to write about and her teacher said her writing often did not flow well, make sense, or come to a reasonable conclusion. In math, Christine seemed dumbfounded when she had to figure out word problems and often failed to get started or come up with a suggestion as to how to solve a problem.

Christine's teachers met on several occasions to think of ways to help her. They tried working with her in small groups, providing step-by-step directions, checking her plan book every day, and, in general, structuring things for her. These methods led to only limited success, so the teacher requested additional information about her levels of achievement and ability.

After completing an assessment, the school psychologist found that the test results were consistent with teacher reports that written expression and math word problems were especially difficult for Christine. The results also indicated that she had particular difficulty with academic tasks required to complete the more complicated assignments, for example, in English and science classes. She could not adequately write and do the math necessary for success. Test results from the Cognitive Assessment System (CAS) also showed that Christine had weak planning processing skills (see Figure 3.1). Christine's PASS Rating Scale, completed by her teacher, also suggested difficulty with planning. Her problem with planning processing was the reason why she had so much trouble doing projects, developing methods for how to complete complex tasks, and monitoring her own progress.

Recommendations for Christine

The school psychologist should select interventions on the basis of two factors. First, Christine needs to be taught specific strategies and plans for composing written work and doing math word problems because her academic problems are related to her planning processing problem. Christine's weakness in planning made it hard for her to do things that require organizing, segmenting the task into portions that can be completed over time, and monitoring her progress. In order to help her be more able to plan while doing these academic tasks, her school psychologist must select handouts for writing and math word problems that use plans or strategies. For example, the handouts Story Plans for Written Composition (p. 97) and Making a Plan for Organizing (p. 65) should be used to help her improve her written work. Christine should be given a lot of opportunity to practice the strategies she was taught, and the teacher or parent should ensure that she uses the strategies.

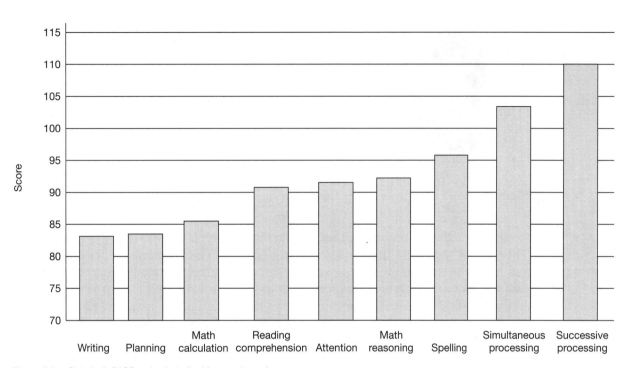

Figure 3.1. Christine's PASS and selected achievement scores.

Second, Christine needs to learn about strategy use and how to plan better. There are some general points that Christine's teachers and parents should remember when teaching her about planning. First, the person helping Christine should be careful to explain exactly what the intervention is, why it is being used, and how it can be helpful for her. Second, the teacher or parent should only provide as much help as is necessary to ensure that she is successful. Christine needs to actively participate in the generation of strategies and determine whether they seem to help. The handouts Teaching Self-Awareness (p. 55) and Teaching Good Thinking Skills (p. 59) are designed for this purpose. In order to help her with her difficulty with math, the handout Planning Facilitation for Math Calculation (p. 109) should be used.

JEREMY'S WEAKNESS IN SIMULTANEOUS PROCESSING

Jeremy was a likeable and social fifth-grade student who paid attention, worked hard, got along well with his peers, and played energetically. Jeremy sat in the middle of the class with a few boys who did well, and he stood out no more than any other student. In fact, a new teacher thought he had no particular difficulties at school, except that he sometimes got frazzled, and she wondered why a previous teacher thought he needed to be retained. What made Jeremy stand out the most was how he often wandered the halls when trying to find a room or person. For the first few weeks of school, he was often late to class because he turned the wrong way

when walking down the hall. Jeremy reported that he did not really understand the layout of the school and tried to walk with a classmate so that he would not get lost.

Jeremy participated minimally in class. He typically answered only when called on. His responses were very simple, and he sometimes provided one confident answer: "I'm not sure." He did his seatwork slowly. Even though he put forth considerable effort, the result was adequate at best. Jeremy could complete homework on an acceptable level, especially handouts and workbook pages that simply required filling in blanks, but he often missed the point because he did not recognize the main ideas or goals of the assignment. He focused on one piece of the task and missed the big picture. Work that required Jeremy to integrate information from a number of sources was simply too difficult for him. For example, he was asked to prepare a poster of himself and his family, including what they like to do. He was excited to complete the class project, and he worked hard at school and home gathering pictures and writing captions. When completed, however, Jeremy's poster was disjointed and unclear. He had a small picture of his family off center with a caption labeling each person. The rest of the poster was filled with athletics pictures and captions about the best team in each professional league. When asked about his poster, Jeremy indicated his father liked professional sports, that he liked college sports, and that the rest of his family did not like sports much at all. The connections between all these events and people were unclear, and his work did not meet the goals of the assignment.

Jeremy did not often ask for help when he needed it because he was not sure what to ask. When he did ask for help or respond to a teacher's offer of help, he said he did not understand, but he could not provide any explanation about what he was confused about. His teachers noted that he really had trouble grasping new concepts and understanding how the new information relates to what he had already learned. Similarly, when doing math word problems, Jeremy had a lot of difficulty understanding what he had to do to get the right answer. He often did not pick out the important parts of the problem and would try to create an equation with all of the numbers given, even when only a few are needed, because he could not separate out the important facts from less important facts.

Jeremy's grades suffered the most when he had to bring together what he had learned for a test or paper. When he studied, he had trouble deciding what exactly he needed to learn and what was important in his textbook. When Jeremy had to review something he had read, he typically just reread the entire passage rather than looking at titles and topic sentences to help him find information. On tests, it was apparent that he did not understand how all of the facts related to each other, and he did not know how to answer test questions, especially ones that require a longer written answer. On tests or activities in which he had to read a passage and answer

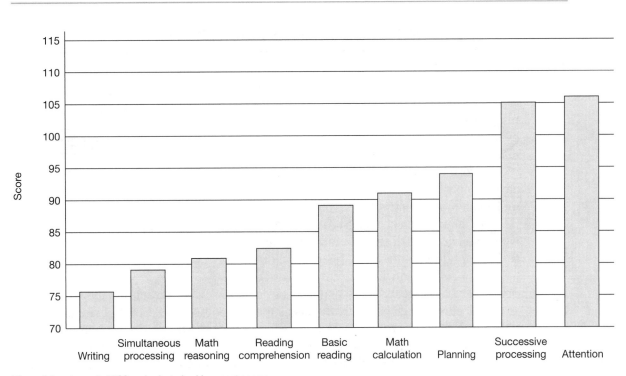

Figure 3.2. Jeremy's PASS and selected achievement scores.

a question, he did not use context clues (which require understanding larger themes) to help him understand unknown words or to infer answers.

Jeremy's school psychologist conducted a thorough assessment and found that Jeremy's test scores were very consistent with what his teachers said about his academic performance (see Figure 3.2). Jeremy's scores on the CAS showed he had a significant weakness in simultaneous processing and similarly poor scores on tests of reading comprehension, writing, and math reasoning.

Recommendations for Jeremy

In order to help Jeremy with these academic tasks, he should be taught to use Story Grammar for Reading Comprehension (p. 77) and Story Grammar for Writing (p. 101), using the appropriate handouts. These interventions will give Jeremy a graphic way of recording relevant information that allows him to more easily see the connections between the ideas. These instructions would help Jeremy see all the facts of a story and how they go together. For math word problems, Jeremy also needs to learn to understand the overall situation being described so that he can separate the important facts from less important facts. The handout Seven-Step Strategy for Math Word Problems (p. 121) is appropriate for Jeremy because it gives him steps to follow to solve the word problems and a specific way to recognize the important facts needed.

BEN'S PROBLEM WITH SUCCESSIVE PROCESSING

Ben was an energetic but frustrated third-grade student who liked his teachers, was popular with his peers, and fit in well socially at school. However, Ben said he did not like school at all, particularly schoolwork. Ben was good at turning in all of his work on time, and he worked hard but he earned poor grades. He appeared to be getting more and more frustrated at school.

In general, Ben struggled to perform well because he had a lot of trouble following directions that were not written down, his writing often did not make sense, and he did not appear to comprehend what he read. Ben's teachers noticed that when directions for assignments and projects were given orally in class, he often only finished part of the task. Ben's teacher described an assignment in which students had to collect insects, label them, organize them into a collection, and then give a brief presentation about each insect. Unlike any other student, Ben chose to make the labels for the insects first and then go look for the insects. He found only a few of the insects he had made labels for and when he put them in the collection, they were not in the order that had been specified. He also had trouble with the spelling of the scientific names of the insects and made many errors in the sequence of letters in the words.

Ben's teachers began to either write up specific directions for Ben or check with him to see whether he had written down the correct tasks and steps. They indicated that this helped, but they still saw him missing parts of assignments. They reported that he continued to talk in class and typically did not express complete thoughts. Similarly, when Ben wrote, he continued to be unable to express his ideas in a logical order, and he sometimes used incorrect tense, conjugation, or number. One of his teachers gave the example that Ben often had trouble filling in blanks on activities in which a paragraph was written but words or sentences were left out. When Ben read short stories and books for reading class, he often remembered the most recent part of the story or other specific parts but did not remember when in the story they happened. His teachers also reported that he routinely related events in a story in the wrong order, so that he came to conclusions that were not logical.

Ben continued to have trouble with math, to the point that his teachers began to allow him to use a calculator regularly. In math class, Ben could do math problems that were on a sheet in front of him. He carefully worked out math problems and used extra space to draw figures or make marks that helped him. When he was asked to solve problems in his head, Ben often had much difficulty, mainly because he could not remember his basic math facts. He usually became quite confused and rarely was able to answer correctly. Ben reported that even though he tried to learn his math facts by writing them repeatedly every day, he could not learn them.

Ben's parents described him as functioning well at home, but before and after school, he would do things around the house in an illogical and inefficient order. For

24

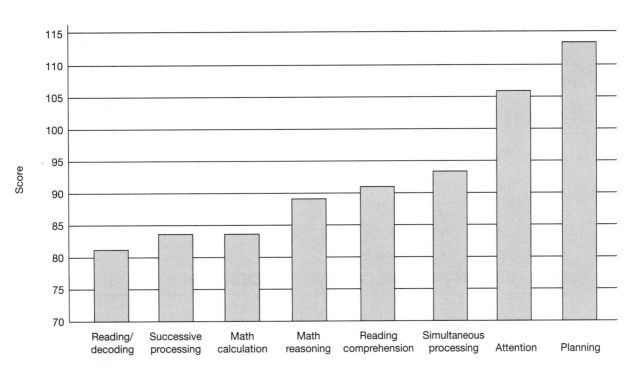

Figure 3.3. Ben's PASS and selected achievement scores.

example, Ben's mother reported that he could not remember telephone numbers very well and wrote the combination for the lock on his bike on his hand. In addition, he had much trouble finding words in a dictionary and did not seem to know the order of letters without singing the alphabet song. Ben's mother considered making checklists for him to follow so that he could complete the tasks in typical routines, such getting ready for bed, in order.

Ben's teachers and parents met with the school psychologist, and they suspected that he had a successive processing problem. They recognized that the skills that are hard for Ben (e.g., following directions, following the order of stories) involved successive processing. The school psychologist tested Ben using the CAS and reported that Ben did, in fact, have a cognitive weakness in successive processing along with low scores in reading and mathematics calculation (see Figure 3.3). Ben's mother completed the PASS Rating Scale, and her ratings also suggested that Ben had poor successive processing. Knowing this, the team decided on a number of methods focused on reading and math that related to successive processing.

Recommendations for Ben

Ben's school psychologist gave his teachers a number of handouts that focused on specific strategies for addressing his academic problems related to successive processing weakness. His teachers plan to use the handout Story Grammar for Reading Comprehension (p. 77) in order to teach Ben to organize what he reads into discrete steps so that he better understands the story's order. They also expect that the handout Plans for Writing (p. 99) will help Ben plan the order of what he writes and that the handout Story Plans for Written Composition (p. 97) will help him write in a way that makes sense. For math, they should teach Ben basic facts using the Number Squares for Math Concepts handout (p. 111) that helps the student see the relationships between numbers. The Plans for Basic Math Facts handout (p. 113) will allow Ben to learn his basic facts through a logical method rather than relying on recall of the sequence of facts. His teachers and parents should encourage him to use these methods whenever he has trouble with math problems. Finally, Ben's teachers must talk to Ben about his weakness and how it relates to his problems in school. They plan to use the Teaching Self-Awareness handout (p. 55) so that he can learn to overcome his weakness and be more successful.

FRANKIE'S WEAKNESSES IN ATTENTION AND SUCCESSIVE PROCESSING

Frankie had trouble in school from the beginning. Although he was friendly and outwardly pleasant, his teachers sensed in him an undercurrent of anxiety and fear that he was not able to perform as well as his peers. Frankie was popular with his sixth-grade teachers because he was very able to converse with them, almost on an adult level, even though he sometimes seemed to miss details in the conversation. His teachers reported that in class, he often looked as if he was not following what was going on. They said he seemed to be "floating, out there somewhere." They also said that "it is like he loses focus for a while, rubs his eyes and covers his ears, but he comes back if you re-direct him." He also became confused when learning, for example, his 20 spelling words each week. So his teachers reduced the number of words he needed to learn to 10. (Later in this discussion, we provide an alternative to this solution.) Frankie's teachers assigned him a peer tutor and group study sessions in addition to class study time. They also encouraged him to tape the lessons, but he reported that it was really hard to listen to them after school.

Frankie said he liked school, but sometimes it was very difficult for him. He performed poorly on tests, especially the ones that required a lot of reading and writing. Homework was also difficult, but fortunately Frankie's parents were very supportive. Each night, they spent several hours working with him on his homework and other assignments. Typically, they helped him read and complete his written work by writing down the answers he provides. Then, he would complete his homework by copying the statements he made that they wrote down for him. His reading, spelling, and writing projects were so difficult that it took a very long time to complete even a simple assignment. Even though he tried hard and his parents helped, Frankie's grades were poor, and he seemed to be getting more and more frustrated at school.

Figure 3.4. Frankie's self-portrait.

Frankie became an anxious and frightened young man. He often had a look of frustration and distress on his face, especially when struggling to do his work. These feelings were well illustrated by the drawing he made of himself, shown in Figure 3.4. This drawing communicates his feelings of being scared and anxious. Frankie's anxiety and fear also led him to be indecisive and unsure of himself. This high level of anxiety contributed to his problems with completing assignments because he often moved from one idea or task to another while talking and then failed to complete his work. At times, he also seemed impatient, restless, and distracted. Even though Frankie was well liked by his teachers, his problems spilled over to his interpersonal relationships with his peers.

Frankie had problems getting along with his peers, who often teased him because he could not keep up with them in class. He was very self-conscious about his academic problems and did not want them to know just how difficult the work was for him. Frankie's interpersonal problems were not, however, just related to academics; they also included sports activities. For example, once when there was a school baseball game, Frankie was playing in the outfield on a sunny, hot day. He was looking at the batter, then the pitcher, then the people in the crowd, then the house behind the people, then the cloud in the sky, then the bird flying by off into the horizon, and he did not even notice that the ball was hit right to him until it nearly hit him in the head. He did not make the catch that would have won the game. Later, he told his parents that he was bored standing out there in the hot sun and did not really like baseball anyway. Of course, this was not exactly how he felt.

Frankie's academic problems in school led his parents to seek the advice of a school psychologist, who discovered that Frankie had considerable problems in cognitive processing, which is related to his academic difficulties. The results also show that Frankie was capable in some areas of PASS (planning and simultaneous processing) and achievement (math calculation and vocabulary) but scored very low in skills related to attention, reading, spelling, and successive processing (see Figure 3.5). This means that Frankie had a primary cognitive weakness in attention and a secondary weakness in successive processing. His reading and spelling scores were similarly low. In Frankie's case, it was clear that his problems with attention and sequencing were at the root of his problems with reading and spelling, which are fundamental to writing in general. Frankie simply could not attend to the words he looked at, the details of the sequence of letters needed for correct spelling, and the order of sound–symbol associations. For example, because of his sequencing problems, he spelled the word *surprise* as *sruprise,* and because he had attention prob-

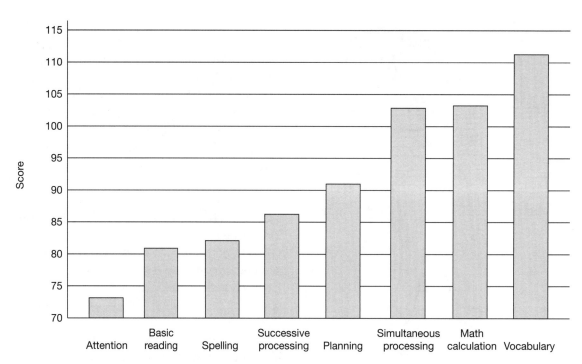

Figure 3.5. Frankie's PASS and selected achievement scores.

lems, he did not notice the sequencing error. His high level of anxiety also played a role here because he was too anxious about the task to spend a lot of time looking closely at the words, and he would rather simply get the task completed and move on. Writing was especially difficult for Frankie because it demanded spelling words correctly, sequencing the words into sentences, and paying attention to how the words and sentences that represent ideas are ordered. Organization of the entire written statement into a properly sequenced story was also very difficult for him. These tasks posed a significant challenge for Frankie.

Recommendations for Frankie

The school psychologists suggested, and his teachers agreed, that several of the methods included in this book were appropriate for Frankie. First, they must teach Frankie about the nature of his attention problem using the handouts Problems with Overcoming Inattention (p. 45) and Improving Attention (p. 63). The methods described in these handouts will help the teacher and Frankie's parents help him understand the challenges he faces with his attention processing weakness and give him options for overcoming these extraordinary demands. This step is very important for Frankie, as it is for many children like him, because it will help him realize that he can be successful despite his cognitive weaknesses and that he is not "stupid," as he has put it. To improve his chances for success, his teachers and parents should also use other handouts such as Strategies for Spelling (p. 95), Plans for Writing (p. 99), and Segmenting Words for Reading/Decoding and Spelling (p. 81).

Finally, one of the most important goals is to teach Frankie ways to improve his attention span and concentration. Before this can happen, however, they must help him recognize when he is not attending and when he is too distracted, using the Self-Monitoring for Planning and Attention Problems handout (pp. 49–50). The complex nature of Frankie's processing weaknesses requires a number of these instructional handouts.

CONCLUSION

This chapter provides case examples to illustrate how the handouts can be used. The procedures we recommend are illustrated in the flow chart presented in Figure 1.1 (page 6) to help the reader determine how a child's problems in school should be addressed. The case studies illustrate how information such as teacher reports, classroom observations, class work, and testing scores can help determine what the child's difficulty may be and which handouts can be used to help. The case studies are not exhaustive, but they are good examples of how to decide which handouts to use and how to help a child learn. In many cases, shifting the cognitive processing demand of the task is an option that helps the child perform the task in a way that does not rely on his or her cognitive weakness. To do this, it will be important to carefully examine the extent to which the PASS processes are involved in the academic task. For example, if the task involves successive processing and the child has difficulty with that cognitive process, it is best to find a method of teaching that does not place so much emphasis on successive processing. Another way to help the student is to teach him or her specific strategies or plans to complete academic tasks. This can help the student learn how to solve problems and become a more effective learner.

References

Kaufman, A.S., & Kaufman, N.L. (1983). *Kaufman Assessment Battery for Children.* Circle Pines: American Guidance Service.

Kroesbergen, E.H., van Luit, J.E.H., & Naglieri, J.A. (in press). *Mathematical learning difficulties and PASS cognitive abilities.* Submitted to Journal of Learning Disabilities.

Luria, A.R. (1966). *Human brain and psychological processes.* New York: Harper & Row.

Luria, A.R. (1973). *The working brain: An introduction to neuropsychology.* New York: Basic Books.

Luria, A.R. (1980). *Higher cortical functions in man* (2nd ed.). New York: Basic Books.

Naglieri, J.A. (1999). *Essentials of CAS assessment.* New York: John Wiley & Sons.

Naglieri, J.A., & Ashman, A.F. (1999). Making the connection between PASS and intervention. In J.A. Naglieri (Ed.), *Essentials of CAS assessment* (pp. 151–181). New York: John Wiley & Sons.

Naglieri, J.A., & Das, J.P. (1997a). *Cognitive Assessment System.* Itasca, IL: Riverside.

Naglieri, J.A., & Das, J.P. (1997b). *Cognitive Assessment System interpretive handbook.* Itasca, IL: Riverside.

Naglieri, J.A., & Gottling, S.H. (1997). Mathematics instruction and PASS cognitive processes: An intervention study. *Journal of Learning Disabilities, 30,* 513–520.

Naglieri, J.A., & Johnson, D. (2000). Effectiveness of a cognitive strategy intervention to improve math calculation based on the PASS theory. *Journal of Learning Disabilities, 33,* 591–597.

Naglieri, J.A., & Rojahn, J.R. (2002). *Validity of the PASS Theory and CAS: Correlations with Achievement.* Submitted to Journal of Educational Psychology.

Peverly, S.T. (1994). An overview of the potential impact of cognitive psychology on school psychology. *School Psychology Review, 23,* 292–309.

Part II

Handouts

Index of Handouts

	Handout	Planning	Attention	Simultaneous processing	Successive processing
PASS	Planning Explained (pp. 37–38)	●			
	Attention Explained (pp. 39–40)		●		
	Simultaneous Processing Explained (pp. 41–42)			●	
	Successive Processing Explained (pp. 43–44)				●
General	Overcoming Problems with Inattention (pp. 45–46)	●			
	Plans for Remembering (pp. 47–48)		●		
	Self-Monitoring for Planning and Attention Problems (pp. 49–50)	●	●		
	Graphic Organizers for Connecting and Remembering Information (pp. 51–52)			●	
	Stop and Think! Teaching Self-Control (pp. 53–54)	●			
	Teaching Self-Awareness (pp. 55–56)	●			
	Promoting Good Listening (p. 57)		●		
	Teaching Good Thinking Skills (pp. 59–60)	●			
	Strategies for Improving Organization (pp. 61–62)	●		●	
	Improving Attention (pp. 63–64)		●		
	Making a Plan for Organizing (p. 65)	●			
Reading	Summarization Strategy for Reading Comprehension (pp. 67–68)			●	
	Plans for Understanding Text (pp. 69–70)	●			
	Plans for Reading Comprehension (pp. 71–72)	●			
	Chunking for Reading/Decoding (p. 73)				●
	Word Families for Reading/Decoding (pp. 75–76)			●	
	Story Grammar for Reading Comprehension (pp. 77–78)				●
	Reading/Decoding Rules (pp. 79–80)				●
	Segmenting Words for Reading/Decoding and Spelling (p. 81)				●
	Letter–Sound Awareness (pp. 83–84)				●
	Plans for Word Syllables (p. 85)				●

	Handout	Planning	Attention	Simultaneous processing	Successive processing
Spelling	Word Sorts for Improving Spelling (p. 87)			●	
	Chunking for Spelling (p. 89)				●
	Letter Ordering for Spelling (pp. 91–92)				●
	Mnemonics for Spelling (pp. 93–94)	●			
	Strategies for Spelling (pp. 95–96)	●			●
Writing	Story Plans for Written Composition (pp. 97–98)				
	Plans for Writing (pp. 99–100)	●			
	Story Grammar for Writing (p. 101)				●
	Teaching Vocabulary Using Visual Cues (p. 103)			●	
	Planning by Writing Sentence Openers (pp. 105–106)	●		●	
	Planning to Write (p. 107)	●			
Math	Planning Facilitation for Math Calculation (pp. 109–110)	●			
	Number Squares for Math Concepts (pp. 111–112)				●
	Plans for Basic Math Facts (pp. 113–114)	●			
	Cuisenaire Rods and Math (pp. 115–116)			●	
	TouchMath for Calculation (pp. 117–118)				●
	Part–Whole Strategy for Math Calculation (pp. 119–120)	●			●
	Seven-Step Strategy for Math Word Problems (pp. 121–122)	●	●	●	●
	Chunking Strategy for Multiplication (pp. 123–124)				●
	Crossed Lines Multiplication Strategy (p. 125)			●	
	More Strategies for Math Word Problems (pp. 127–128)	●	●	●	●
Test taking	General Strategies for Test Taking (p. 129)	●			
	Strategies for Multiple Choice, Matching, and True–False Tests (p. 131)	●			
	Strategies for Written Tests (p. 133)	●			

Planning Explained

Planning is a mental process by which the individual determines, selects, applies, and evaluates solutions to problems. This includes 1) selecting relevant information in the task, 2) selecting relevant prior knowledge, 3) using a strategy to approach a task, 4) monitoring progress, and 5) developing new strategies when necessary.

Example of Planning in the Classroom

Figure 1 shows a classroom activity that involves planning. A common task for children is learning to spell words correctly. Teachers often give students spelling tests on specific lists of words. There are a many ways for a child to memorize a spelling list. In this example, the child is encouraged to use a plan or method to learn to spell a list of words. Writing the list in alphabetical order, making flashcards, writing the words in sentences, writing the list every day, and simply reading over the list are a few ways children may learn words. Some of these plans are better for some children than other plans. Selecting of one of these methods, applying it, seeing if it works, and changing it if it does not is good planning. A child who plans how to do a task and monitors how well the strategy works is likely to be more successful than a child who does a task without a plan.

This Week's Spelling Words

Here are the words for this Friday's test:

1. found
2. ground
3. mouth
4. ouch
5. couch
6. count
7. round
8. out
9. shout
10. north
11. south
12. east
13. west
14. globe
15. robe

How will you learn the words?

1. Start today
2. Study 15 minutes per day
3. Study with a friend
4. Write each word 10 times
5. Make flashcards
6. Make a word search puzzle

What other ways to learn these words can you think of? Write them down!

_____

_____

_____

Figure 1. An example of a classroom activity that requires planning processing.

Planning describes several kinds of things:

- Making decisions about how to do things
- Evaluating the environment to determine how a problem or task could be solved
- Developing, selecting, evaluating, and using plans or strategies to solve problems
- Modifying plans or strategies to be more efficient
- Determining when the task has been completed appropriately
- Controlling behavior, impulses, and mental activity
- Defining a problem (the need for plan) and selecting and applying a plan to solve a problem (completing a task).

There are several classroom problems related to planning:

- Disorganized completion of assignments
- Failure to switch strategies according to the demands of school work
- Failure to correct misinterpretation of what is read
- Inconsistent application of spelling or math rules when solving problems
- Failure to devise or use aids when completing work
- Lack of preparedness with materials needed to do school work
- Uncertainty about how or where to start school work

How to Teach Students Better Planning Skills

1. Teach children about plans and strategy use.
2. Discuss the importance of planning in class, how it helps students organize themselves so that they can be more successful and finish on time.
3. Encourage children to develop, use, and evaluate their own strategies.
4. Encourage verbalization of ideas and strategies.
5. Explain why some methods work better than others.
6. Ask questions related to planning, such as
   - "How did you do the task?"
   - "Did you make a plan before you started the task?"
   - "What did you do last time? Did it work?"
   - "Why did you do it that way?"
   - "These are hard. Is there a way to make them easier?"
   - "Is there a better way, or is there another way to do this?"
   - "What strategy worked for you?"
   - "Do you think you will do anything differently next time?"
   - "How can you check your work to see if it is right?"

How Is Planning Measured?

Planning can be measured using the Cognitive Assessment System (CAS). The CAS gives an overall score and separate PASS scores for the four cognitive scales, including planning. The average score is 100. Children who earn scores below 90 are considered below average.

Resources

Kirby, J.R., & Williams, N.H. (1991). *Learning problems: A cognitive approach*. Toronto: Kagan & Woo Limited.
Naglieri, J.A. (1999). *Essentials of CAS assessment*. New York: John Wiley & Sons.
Naglieri, J.A., & Das, J.P. (1997). *Cognitive Assessment System*. Itasca, IL: Riverside.

Attention Explained

Attention is a mental process by which the person focuses his or her thinking on a particular stimulus and ignores others. Attention allows a child to selectively focus on things heard or seen and resist being distracted by irrelevant sights and sounds. Focused attention is direct concentration on something. Selective attention involves the resistance to distraction, and sustained attention is continued focus over time. These dimensions work together to allow a child to attend.

Example of Attention in the Classroom

Children often take multiple choice tests, which include problems with a list of possible answers. In the worksheet shown in Figure 1, a child must focus on the specific question or problem and examine the options carefully. The child must focus on the correct answer while at the same time ignoring the other answers that are wrong but may be quite close to the correct answer. One math problem asks "What is the number for 5 tens and 2 ones?" and lists 50, 25, 52, 502, and 55 as possible answers. This problem contains several distracting options. The 2 can be in any location, but is that location the tens place? This creates a situation with targets (the tens place) and distracters (the ones or hundreds place). The "respond" or "do-not-respond" situation demands selective attention and resistance to distraction. Similarly, attention is needed in the classroom when a student must selectively focus on the teacher in the front of the room while ignoring the noises in the hall, the students playing outside, and the student next to him or her.

Attention describes a number of activities:

- Focusing on one stimulus at a time
- Resisting distractions
- Sustaining effort over time
- Paying selective attention to one thing to the exclusion of others
- Maintaining focus over time

Here are some classroom problems related to attention:

- Limited ability to work for more than a few minutes on one thing
- Failure to focus on relevant aspects of assignments
- Difficulty in resisting distractions in the classroom
- Incomplete work because the child did not sustain the effort

---

Math Worksheet for Tens and Ones

Name: _____   Date: _____

Circle the correct answers.

1. What is the number for 5 tens and 2 ones?

    50   25   52   502   55

2. Which number has a 2 in the tens place and a 7 in the ones place?

    27   270   72   22   702

3. Which number has a 5 in the tens place and a 4 in the ones place?

    504   54   55   45   50

4. Which number has a 6 in the tens place and a 9 in the ones place?

    66   690   96   69   996

Figure 1. An example of an activity that requires attention processing.

- Tendency to answer questions based on incomplete information
- Tendency to answer the wrong question
- Failure to start a task because the instructions were missed

Strategies for Developing Attention

- Model and teach strategies that improve attention and concentration.
- Teach the use of verbal self-commands (e.g., "Okay, calm down and think about the question").
- Teach focusing strategies (e.g., checking for critical features and careful listening).
- Teach the child to use only required materials.
- Teach strategies that increase inhibition and organization.
- Encourage the use of date books and special notebooks for organizing papers.
- Teach the child to stop and think before responding.
- Teach the child to count to 10 before answering.
- Teach strategies to increase alertness.
- Teach the child to be aware of his or her level of alertness.
- Teach the child to use calming self-statements.
- Encourage planned breaks so that the child does not have to sustain his or her effort for too long.

How Is Attention Measured?

Attention can be measured using the Cognitive Assessment System (CAS). The CAS gives an overall score and separate PASS scores for the four cognitive scales, including attention. The average score is 100. Children who earn scores below 90 are considered below average.

Resources

Kirby, J.R. & Williams, N.H. (1991). *Learning problems: A cognitive approach.* Toronto: Kagan & Woo Limited.

Naglieri, J.A. (1999). *Essentials of CAS assessment.* New York: John Wiley & Sons.

Naglieri, J.A., & Das, J.P. (1997). *Cognitive Assessment System.* Itasca, IL: Riverside.

Pressley, M., & Woloshyn, V. (1995). *Cognitive strategy instruction that really improves children's academic performance* (2nd ed.). Cambridge, MA: Brookline Books.

Simultaneous Processing Explained

Simultaneous processing is a mental process used to relate separate pieces of information as a group or see how parts are related to a whole. Usually simultaneous processing is seen in tasks that involve spatial skills such as using blocks to build a design, doing geometry, seeing patterns in numbers, seeing a group of letters as a word, understanding words as a whole, understanding a sentence as part of a paragraph, and reading comprehension. The spatial aspect of simultaneous processing includes the perception of an object as a whole and seeing patterns. Simultaneous processing is involved in reading comprehension in that it requires the integration and understanding of word relationships, prepositions, and inflections so that a person can derive meaning based on the whole idea. Children good at simultaneous processing easily recognize themes and how facts fit together to form a complete whole.

Example of Simultaneous Processing in the Classroom

Simultaneous processing is involved in the comprehension of spoken and written language. For example, the sentence "The black cat ran" requires a student to relate the element "cat" with the element "blackness" and relate it to the action "run." Grouping the words, "flowers," "birds," "rocks," and "clouds" into a group of "things you can find outside" uses simultaneous processing because it requires one to see how each of those things relates to each other and to the statement.

Simultaneous processing is required for things to be seen as a whole. To recognize a shape in a collection of lines that form a cube requires simultaneous processing, as does drawing a map (see Figure 1). Drawing or making a map requires grasping the relationship of one place to another in a meaningful way, rather than seeing a map as a bunch of shapes and lines.

A simple but common task for children in school is to draw pictures, often pictures about a story they have written or read. Simply drawing the picture and seeing how each part, color, and design fits to make the artwork meaningful requires simultaneous processing. A drawing that includes all of the necessary parts in a well-organized group involves simultaneous processing. Relating the picture to what was read or written requires the student to understand the story and how its parts are interrelated.

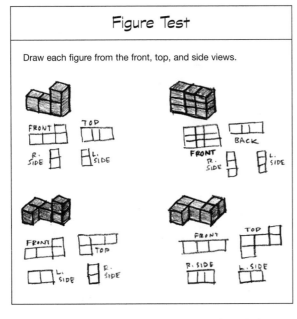

Figure Test

Draw each figure from the front, top, and side views.

Figure 1. An example of an activity that requires simultaneous processing.

Simultaneous processing describes several activities:

- Relating parts into a comprehensive whole to see how things fit together
- Understanding relationships among words, pictures, or ideas
- Working with spatial relationships
- Seeing several things or integrating words into a larger idea

Here are some classroom problems related to simultaneous processing:

- Failure to recognize sight words quickly
- Failure to interpret word, sentence, or passage meaning
- Difficulty with seeing the shapes of words or working with spatial tasks
- Failure to see patterns in text or math problems
- Failure to comprehend math word problems

Strategies for Developing Simultaneous Processing

- Do matching and categorization games (e.g., pictures, words), including opposites, with the child
- Show the child reproduction of figures in rotation and from different perspectives
- Have the child practice on jigsaw puzzles, hidden picture worksheets, and building three-dimensional objects
- Ask the child to supply missing details in stories
- Encourage rhyming
- Have the child use and create of maps, both geographical and contextual
- Teach the child how to summarize stories or articles

How Is Simultaneous Processing Measured?

Simultaneous processing can be measured using the Cognitive Assessment System (CAS). The CAS gives an overall score and separate PASS scores for the four cognitive scales, including planning. The average score is 100. Children who earn scores below 90 are considered below average.

Resources

Kirby, J.R., & Williams, N.H. (1991). *Learning problems: A cognitive approach.* Toronto: Kagan & Woo Limited.
Naglieri, J.A. (1999). *Essentials of CAS assessment.* New York: John Wiley & Sons.
Naglieri, J.A., & Das, J.P. (1997). *Cognitive Assessment System.* Itasca, IL: Riverside.

Successive Processing Explained

Successive processing is a mental process involved in using or putting information in a specific order. In this process, incoming information is organized in order so that the only connections are the links of one part to the next, which allows a child to see how parts are sequenced. This process is important when it is necessary to keep information in its correct order. For example, children who are good successive processors are usually able to follow verbal instructions well. Successive processing involves remembering information in order, including the order of sounds and movements. For this reason, successive processing is used when blending sounds to form words and putting words in the correct syntactical order.

Example of Successive Processing in the Classroom

Successive processing is involved when children work with sounds in order to form words. Children learn to speak by putting the correct sounds of words into the correct order. They learn the sequences of sounds used to make words before they begin to read. When they begin to learn to read, the sounds of the words are important and so is the association of those sounds with sequences of letters. Therefore, reading/decoding involves successive processing. In Figure 1, the child must sequence the correct sounds in order to say the phrase "Arty ate apples," put the words in the correct order, and put the words the letters used to spell these words in the correct order. The similarity of the words (all begin with the letter a) makes this difficult. Because sequencing of sounds is involved in reading, a related example is found in spelling. Successive processing is involved in spelling because the child must produce the correct sequence of letters to form a word (e.g., "h-o-u-s-e").

Learning basic math facts requires successive processing if the child is instructed to learn by repeatedly writing the facts. The child who writes "8 + 9 = 17" is being taught a specific string of numbers, which requires successive processing. The completion of more complex math also involves successive processing. For example, completing the equation "3(3 + 7) – 12 = x" requires following a specific sequence of operations (add, multiply, subtract) to arrive at the right answer. A child who has trouble remembering basic math facts or the order of math procedures is likely have a weakness in successive processing.

Words with Similar Sounds

Name: _____   Date: _____

Copy each sentence carefully.

1. Arty ate apples.

_____

2. Larry lost his little lock.

_____

3. She sees sea shells by the sea.

_____

4. Betty bought a box of baseballs.

_____

Figure 1.   An example of an activity that requires successive processing.

Successive processing is involved in several kinds of activities:

- Working with things in specific order (e.g., ordering sounds or words)
- Understanding facts based on order
- Perceiving stimuli in a sequence
- Executing movements in order
- Remembering and holding sounds or words in sequences
- Retaining sequences of events from text and serial organization of speech

Here are some problems related to successive processing:

- Poor word decoding skills
- Failure to comprehend syntax structure
- Failure to pronounce words and sequence word segments accurately
- Difficulty with following steps or tendency to omit steps needed to solve problems
- Lack of comprehension of the sequence of events in a story

Strategies for Developing Successive Processing

- Teach the child to organize things in steps as a strategy for completing tasks.
- Say and write alphabet letters or numbers in order.
- Memorize poems, songs, or lines in a play (and make it fun).
- Arrange items or repeat events from a story or occasion in order.
- Follow specific, ordinal instructions.
- Write out steps of an everyday activity.

How Is Successive Processing Measured?

Successive processing can be measured using the Cognitive Assessment System (CAS). The CAS gives an overall score and separate PASS scores for the four cognitive scales, including successive processing. The average score is 100. Children who earn scores below 90 are considered below average.

Resources

Kirby, J.R., & Williams, N.H. (1991). *Learning problems: A cognitive approach.* Toronto: Kagan & Woo Limited.
Naglieri, J.A. (1999). *Essentials of CAS assessment.* New York: John Wiley & Sons.
Naglieri, J.A., & Das, J.P. (1997a). *Cognitive Assessment System.* Itasca, IL: Riverside.

From **Helping Children Learn: Intervention Handouts for Use in School and at Home** by Jack A. Naglieri, Ph.D., and Eric B. Pickering, Ph.D. © 2003 Paul H. Brookes Publishing Co.; 1-800-638-3775; www.brookespublishing.com

Overcoming
Problems with Inattention

Attention is the process a person uses to focus thinking on a particular stimulus while ignoring others. Throughout a school day, a student must pay attention to the teacher, the instructions being given, what must be done, and what specific materials are needed, while ignoring other students talking, the students playing outside the window, and the cart rolling by in the hall. Attention processes allow a child to selectively focus on things heard or seen and resist being distracted by irrelevant sights and sounds. *Focused attention* is direct concentration on something, such as a specific math problem. *Selective attention* involves the resistance to distraction such as listening to the teacher and not the cart in the hall. *Sustained attention* is continued focus over time.

Some children have difficulty with focused thinking and resisting distractions. These children fit the description of attention-deficit/hyperactivity disorder (ADHD), predominantly inattentive type (American Psychiatric Association, 2000). Children with the inattentive type of ADHD are different from those with ADHD, predominantly hyperactive-impulsive type, described by Barkley (1994) as a delay in the development of inhibition, disturbed self-regulation, and poor organization over time. Children with ADHD, hyperactive-impulsive type cannot control their behavior and have inattention problems that are related to a failure in the process of planning on the CAS.

How to Help a Child
Overcome Problems with Inattention

The first step is to help the child understand the nature of their attention problems, including

1. Concepts such as attention, resistance to distraction, and control of attention
2. Recognition of how attention affects daily functioning
3. Recognition that the deficit can be overcome
4. Basic elements of the control program

Second, teachers and parents can help the child improve his or her motivation and persistence:

1. Promote success via small steps
2. Ensure success at school and at home
   - Allow for oral responses to tests
   - Circumvent reading whenever possible
3. Teach rules for approaching tasks
   - Help the child to define tasks accurately
   - Assess the child's knowledge of problems
   - Encourage the child to consider all possible solutions

- Teach the child to use a correct test strategy (Pressley & Woloshyn, 1995, p. 140)

4. Discourage passivity and encourage independence
   - Provide only as much assistance as is needed
   - Reduce the use of teacher solutions only
   - Require the child to take responsibility for correcting his or her own work
   - Help the child to become more self-reliant

5. Encourage the child to avoid
   - Excessive talking
   - Working fast with little accuracy
   - Giving up too easily
   - Turning in sloppy disorganized papers

Third, teachers and parents should give the child specific problem-solving strategies:

1. Model and teach strategies that improve attention and concentration.
2. Help the child to recognize when he or she is under- or overattentive.

Who Should Receive Help with Overcoming Problems with Inattention?

This instruction benefits students who have problems maintaining attention and/or who are overactive. These strategies may be particularly helpful for children who demonstrate low scores in attention and children who show weaknesses in attention along with problems with planning. Because a student that has a planning weakness may have a particularly difficult time monitoring and controlling his or her actions, these strategies may be useful to provide structure and help the student follow specific plans to increase his or her self-control and focus of attention.

Resources

Sources for information on attention problems and other educational problems can be found at www.hood.edu/seri/serihome.html/, www.chadd.com/, and www.iss.stthomas.edu/studyguides/adhd.htm/.

American Psychiatric Association. (1994). *Diagnostic and statistical manual of mental disorders* (4th ed., text rev.) Washington, DC: Author.

Barkley, R.A., & Murphy, K.R. (1998). *Attention deficit hyperactivity disorder: A clinical workbook* (2nd ed.) New York: The Guilford Press.

Naglieri, J.A. (1999). *Essentials of CAS assessment.* New York: John Wiley & Sons.

Pressley, M., & Woloshyn, V. (1995). *Cognitive strategy instruction that really improves children's academic performance* (2nd ed.). Cambridge, MA: Brookline Books.

Welton, E. (1999). How to help inattentive students find success in school: Getting the homework back from the dog. *Teaching Exceptional Children, 31,* 12–18.

Plans for Remembering

Memorizing facts is an important part of school learning. Many times, children recite facts, such 8 + 9 = 17, which requires understanding the order of the numbers because of their arrangement. Memory strategies (e.g., a plan) are an excellent way to help children remember facts they need to know because the strategies change the way children think about or process the information. Memory or mnemonic strategies are techniques for increasing learning to help long-term memory of important information. When people read facts, they are better able to remember them later when the facts are made more meaningful through their relationship to other things already known and through elaboration. Mnemonics is a specific strategy for doing this.

Mnemonics

Figure 1 illustrates how a child who has difficulty remembering the order of math operations can use a memory strategy (i.e., a plan). In this example, the mnemonic device allows the child to perform the operations in the correct order by using the strategy rather than by relying on the memory of the sequence of operations. Other plans for remembering include associations of pictures with a word.

How to Teach Plans for Remembering

The *keyword method* is a plan for remembering that enhances learning by helping the individual organize incoming information for better storage and retrieval. Following are steps for using the keyword method to remember new vocabulary words.

1. The child associates a new word to a familiar word. For example, *ranid* (which means *frog*) is matched to similar sounding word, *rain*.
2. The child remembers that keyword for *ranid* is *rain*.
3. The child relates the keyword to the unfamiliar word's meaning. For example, frogs like water, so they like rain.
4. The child makes mental image of a frog in the rain.
5. The child retrieves the new word's meaning. For example, the child might think, "What does *ranid* mean? It sounds like rain, and I remember the image of a frog in the rain. *Ranid* means *frog.*"

Who Should Be Taught Plans for Remembering?

Plans for remembering appear most useful for memorization of specific words or facts, for the sciences, history, foreign languages, rules for writing, math facts, and so forth. Children who perform poorly in successive processing often have trouble with remembering facts based on the order of information. This instruction benefits students who are poor in successive processing and students who score low in planning because it gives them a strategy or plan for remembering.

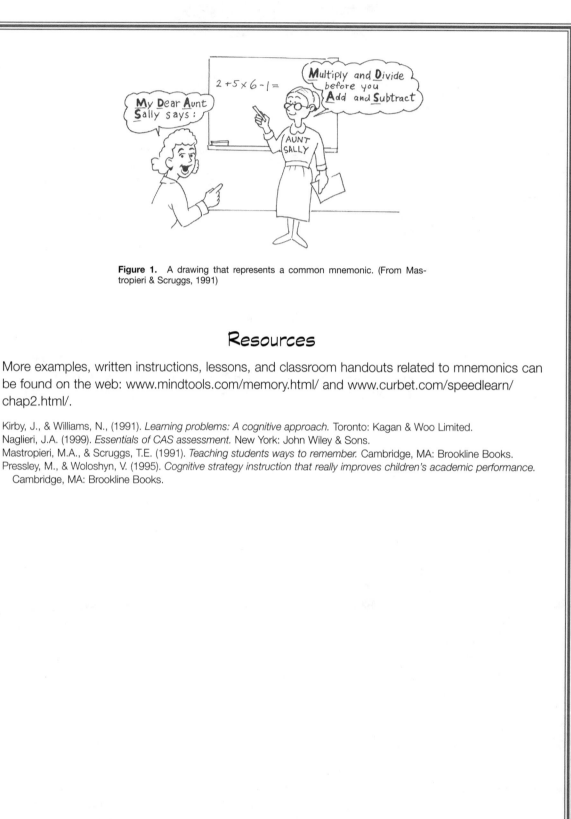

Figure 1. A drawing that represents a common mnemonic. (From Mastropieri & Scruggs, 1991)

Resources

More examples, written instructions, lessons, and classroom handouts related to mnemonics can be found on the web: www.mindtools.com/memory.html/ and www.curbet.com/speedlearn/chap2.html/.

Kirby, J., & Williams, N., (1991). *Learning problems: A cognitive approach.* Toronto: Kagan & Woo Limited.

Naglieri, J.A. (1999). *Essentials of CAS assessment.* New York: John Wiley & Sons.

Mastropieri, M.A., & Scruggs, T.E. (1991). *Teaching students ways to remember.* Cambridge, MA: Brookline Books.

Pressley, M., & Woloshyn, V. (1995). *Cognitive strategy instruction that really improves children's academic performance.* Cambridge, MA: Brookline Books.

Self-Monitoring for
Planning and Attention Problems

Children who behave well and are successful in the classroom must manage their own behavior by attending to the teacher, concentrating on the task at hand, and monitoring and adjusting their own social and academic behavior. To do this, a child must be able to focus attention on what is relevant, resist distraction by irrelevant things, and monitor and evaluate how they are doing. Some children, however, have a difficult time with controlling their behavior. They are easily distracted and often off task, and they are limited in their strategic approaches to controlling their own behavior. Teachers can use a strategy called *self-monitoring* to help students control their own behavior.

Self-Monitoring

Self-monitoring is a technique used to help children monitor their productivity (how *much* they have completed in a given time) and their accuracy (how *correct* they are in a given time) during the school day. Self-monitoring academic performance increases the amount of on-task behavior by children who are typically off-task. It helps children focus on what they need to be doing and whether they are doing it. Even when the self-monitoring task is related to specific school work, better behavior usually results.

How to Teach Self-Monitoring

This section describes the use of self-monitoring to affect academic performance, but the strategy may be modified so that the students are randomly signaled several times during a session to record if they are on-task or not (after explicit and positive descriptions of what on-task behavior is). The teacher should follow these steps:

1. Provide specific description of academic accuracy and academic productivity.
2. Hand out a record sheet, and explain that at the end of each session the child is to record the number of items completed with the total number of items given (productivity) and the number of items correct with the total number of items given (accuracy) in the appropriate columns (see Figure 1).
3. Explain that self-monitoring is important for on-task behavior and successful learning and demonstrate how to calculate and record the percentages for accuracy and productivity at the end of the session (10- to 30-minute period).
4. Provide a session in which the students work on a task with a specific number of items (e.g., spelling list, math problems, question sheets related to a story). It is acceptable for students at different levels to have different activities.
5. At the end of the session, have students record and calculate their progress.
6. Have students keep daily logs, and encourage students to compare percentages of previous sessions to recent sessions. Teachers may choose to have students graph

My Work Log						
Date	Number finished	Total number	Percentage	Number correct	Total number	Percentage

Figure 1. A sample record sheet for self-monitoring.

their own progress or to post a graph in class charting the productivity and accuracy of individual students or the whole class. Reinforcement or rewards are not necessary, but some teachers do choose to reward students for certain levels of success.

Throughout these steps the teacher should model self-recording and monitoring, provide feedback, allow students to independently record their performance, encourage students to examine their performance over time, praise accurate self-reporting, and be patient—success may not come immediately.

Who Should Learn Self-Monitoring?

The self-monitoring strategy is helpful for students who need to learn to be more productive in class. Children who are inattentive or who score low in planning processing are likely to need to learn self-monitoring strategies for doing schoolwork (Naglieri, 1999).

Resources

Naglieri, J.A. (1999). *Essentials of CAS assessment.* New York: John Wiley & Sons.

Graphic Organizers for Connecting and Remembering Information

Remembering and relating information is a common part of learning and daily life. Students are often expected to learn large amounts of new and unfamiliar information. Learning facts requires the student to see how information is connected or related. Students often remember this information better if they see it graphically and understand how it relates to knowledge they already have. Graphic organizers are designed to help students (and teachers) present and organize information so it is easier to understand and remember.

Graphic Organizers

New information is better remembered if it is connected to information the students already know. *Graphic organizers* are visual representations of information that shows the links of new information to other new and existing information. This makes the new information easier to understand and learn. Furthermore, the visual nature of graphic organizers and the links they make help students understand the connections between information parts. For example, a graphic organizer might be used to teach young children about different animals. A child learning about different kinds of animals might already know what a fish is. This knowledge can be used to graphically organize whales, sharks, and dolphins. They all live underwater, but sharks have gills and are fish. (Whales and dolphins have blowholes and breathe air, so they are not fish.) Figure 1 represents one way to map this graphically.

Another type of graphic organizer is a Venn diagram, which uses circles to demonstrate how concepts are related. Figure 2 shows the same information as Figure 1 in the form of a Venn diagram.

How to Teach Graphic Organizers

Graphic organizers are fairly simple to create. They need not be reserved for factual information. They can be used for activities such as exploring creative concepts, organizing writing, and developing language skills. Four steps to follow in creating a graphic organizer are

1. Select information that you need to present to the child (which may be from a story, a chapter, or any concepts).
2. Determine the key components that are necessary for the child to learn.
3. Create the graphic representation of the information. The illustration should include

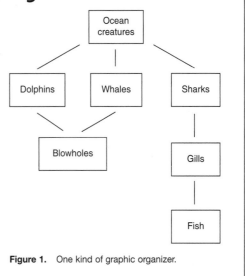

Figure 1. One kind of graphic organizer.

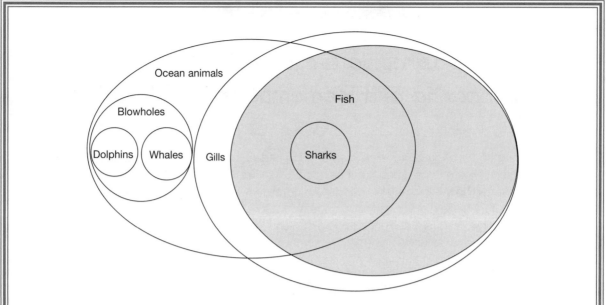

Figure 2. Another kind of graphic organizer.

    the key concepts, concepts the child already knows, and the linkages between the concepts.

4. Present the organizer to the child and discuss it to be sure he or she understands the information and sees the connections.

    Students may also be taught to develop their own graphic organizers as a strategy to help them understand and learn information independently.

Who Should Learn Graphic Organizers?

Students who have trouble learning new information or organizing information may find graphic organizers helpful. Students who score low in simultaneous processing have trouble understanding how information is related and may find graphic organizers particularly helpful. They may also be helpful for students who score low in planning (Naglieri, 1999) as a strategy to help them organize information.

Resources

Two excellent resources are found at www.tld.jcu.edu.au/netshare/learn/mindmap/ and www.iss.stthomas.edu/studyguides/mapping.htm/.

Dye, G.A. (2000). Graphic organizer to the rescue, helping students link and remember information. *The Council For Exceptional Children, 32*(3), 72–76.
Naglieri, J.A. (1999). *Essentials of CAS assessment.* New York: John Wiley & Sons.

Stop and Think!
Teaching Self-Control

Students who behave well use self-control to think about what they are doing and change their behavior if it is not okay. For some students, self-control is natural. These students actively monitor their behavior, determine if what they are doing or going to do is okay, and change it if it is not. If they decide their behavior will not be acceptable, they think about other options and choose the best one. This requires that the student be aware of his or her own behavior and understand that behavior relative to the rules or his or her own goals. Stop and Think! is intended to teach students a plan to help them control their behavior.

Some students act inappropriately because they have not monitored their behavior, selected the best way to act from their options, or even realized they have other options. To help these students, explicitly teach them that they need to monitor and control their behavior, to stop and think about their behavior, and then give them a plan for doing so.

How To Teach Stop and Think!

To encourage positive self-control, students should be first directly taught to pay attention to and think about their behavior. Teachers can first explicitly teach the student that when the phrase "Stop and think!" is said, the student should think about what he or she is doing. The student then should be taught to ask him- or herself appropriate questions about actions, such as "What am I doing?" and, "Is what I'm doing okay?" If the child is about to do something, the questions "What do I want to do?" and, "Is what I want to do okay?" may be posed. Initially, these questions could be put on the student's desk or posted on the wall as a reminder.

The student may be given the following plan to follow to determine what is going on in a situation, think about what his or her options are, and choose the best one.

1. Stop and think.
2. Identify the situation.
3. Ask, "What do I want to do?"
4. Ask, "Is there a problem?"
5. Ask, "What are possible solutions?"
6. Consider the consequences to each solution.
7. Choose the best solution.
8. Evaluate the results.

Each of these steps should be explicitly taught and discussed so that the student understands what to do for each step.

From **Helping Children Learn: Intervention Handouts for Use in School and at Home** by Jack A. Naglieri, Ph.D.,
and Eric B. Pickering, Ph.D. © 2003 Paul H. Brookes Publishing Co.; 1-800-638-3775; www.brookespublishing.com

Who Should Be Taught Stop and Think?

Students with difficult behavior are likely to benefit from being taught to stop and think. Students who have a planning weakness may have a particularly difficult time monitoring and controlling their actions (Naglieri, 1999). This technique may be used to help the student follow a specific plan to increase his or her self-control.

Resources

Ashman, A.F., & Conway, R.N.F. (1997). *An introduction to cognitive education.* London: Routledge.

Naglieri, J.A. (1999). *Essentials of CAS assessment.* New York: John Wiley & Sons.

Teaching Self-Awareness

Successful learners know how to study well, use good and appropriate learning strategies that help them remember better, and regulate their own activity. These students are aware that, depending on the task, some ways to learn may be better than others. Good learners are aware of the demands of the learning task and select a good way to complete the task. Self-awareness and ability to choose appropriate strategies involve forethought and planning. For some students, explicit instruction to be self-aware of one's own learning is necessary. This intervention is intended to help students learn successfully by being more self-aware.

Self-Awareness

Many students with academic problems are not aware of how their behavior can influence their own learning. They may lack the self-awareness that more successful learners have. These students often seem disorganized and unsure of how to approach a learning task. These types of students must be directly taught to be self-aware and to use strategies for better learning.

How to Teach Self-Awareness

In general, students must be made aware of the importance of learning strategies. Educators should teach knowledge of learning by discussing that

- Students can do some things that help them remember better
- People sometimes forget things they have learned
- Some things are more difficult to remember
- People forget things for different reasons
- Attention and effort have roles in improving memory
- Repetition can be helpful
- Knowing and using strategies can be very helpful

Teachers should spend time discussing with students their methods for learning tasks and what ways are better than others. Students should be instructed to pay attention to the learning situation. In other words, students should ask themselves:

- "What is the reason for doing this?"
- "Have I done something like this before?"
- "What are the different ways I can do this?"
- "What is the best way to do this?"

Students can also be instructed to evaluate what they are doing while they are doing it:

- "Is this strategy working?"
- "Is there another way I can do this that is better?"
- "Is this working for me?"

Recognizing the importance of using specific strategies is critical because at first, strategies may not seem worth the effort. Using strategies can be encouraged by giving regular positive feedback when the student is using a strategy, by highlighting when a student was successful because a strategy was used, and attributing failure to the lack of strategy use. When students realize they have some control over their success through strategy use, they are more likely to be self-aware and to use strategies. Furthermore, if a teacher regularly uses and models a strategy, students are more likely to use it themselves.

Who Should Be Taught Self-Awareness?

Most students can benefit from being taught good self-awareness. Students who score low in planning may benefit even more from direct instruction and strategies in self awareness (Naglieri, 1999).

Resources

Corral, N., & Shirin, A.D. (1997, March/April) Self talk strategies for success in math. *The Council For Exceptional Children.* 42–45.

Kirby, J.R., & Williams, N.H. (1991). *Learning problems: A cognitive approach.* Toronto: Kagan & Woo Limited.

Naglieri, J.A. (1999). *Essentials of CAS assessment.* New York: John Wiley & Sons.

Pressley, M., & Woloshyn, V. (1995). *Cognitive strategy instruction that really improves children's academic performance.* Cambridge, MA: Brookline Books.

Promoting Good Listening

Teachers provide most of their instruction and directions orally, which means that good listening skills are critical for all students. Being a good listener requires being able to follow along, understand what is expected, and understand what is being taught. Some students do not have good listening skills. These students need to be specifically taught good listening skills, be given opportunities to practice listening skills with feedback, and be provided an environment that encourages good listening.

Children who are effective listeners are better able to receive the information presented to them. They look at their teacher during instruction, actively listen to what is being said, and connect what they hear to their understanding of the topic. Good listeners understand cues in speech (e.g., first, second, third; "The next important step is . . .") and use those cues to focus their attention. This strategy is intended to provide the teacher with some approaches to help promote good listening in students.

How to Teach Good Listening

Teachers can do the following to promote good listening:

1. Be sure the students can hear, taking into account hearing ability as well as seat placement.
2. Explain the purpose of listening.
3. Specifically teach and use organizational cues.
4. Use phrases such as "this is important" and "make sure you remember this."
5. Describe specific verbal and nonverbal cues that highlight important information (e.g., when the teacher explains something and writes it on the board).
6. Use students' names during direct instruction.
7. Vary the teaching pace.
8. Write important parts, directions, and connectors on the board.
9. Give students advanced organizers so that they know what to expect and listen for.
10. Prompt students to generate questions before the lecture and listen for the answers.
11. Have students relate the presentation to their own experience and knowledge.
12. Provide students with partial outlines in which they must listen and fill in the blanks.
13. Stop regularly to verify that students understand what is going on and have them summarize the main points.

From **Helping Children Learn: Intervention Handouts for Use in School and at Home** by Jack A. Naglieri, Ph.D., and Eric B. Pickering, Ph.D. © 2003 Paul H. Brookes Publishing Co.; 1-800-638-3775; www.brookespublishing.com

Who Should Be Taught Good Listening?

All students can benefit from being taught good listening skills. Teaching and supporting good listening skills is particularly helpful for students who score low in attention (Naglieri, 1999) and may also be helpful for students who score low in planning.

Resources

Mastropieri, M.A., & Scruggs, T.E. (2000). *The inclusive classroom: Strategies for effective instruction.* Upper Saddle River, NJ: Merrill.

Naglieri, J.A. (1999). *Essentials of CAS assessment.* New York: John Wiley & Sons.

Teaching Good Thinking Skills

Information is learned better when it is carefully and thoroughly examined and especially when it is connected to what is already known. For example, it is easier to remember a new person's name if it is the same as your own or someone close to you. In this case, the new name is easier to remember because it relates to something you are already familiar with. Successful students know that thoroughly thinking about a new topic helps them learn more and helps them learn the material better. Students who are thoughtful learners are usually aware that carefully reflecting and relating new information to old helps them learn the information better. Those students who have good thinking skills know how to study well, use good and appropriate learning strategies that help them remember better, and regulate their own activity.

Some students need to be taught to think closely, examine new information, and relate to things already known to help them learn better—that is, they need to learn thinking skills. These students may have academic problems because they are not aware of the need to have good thinking skills in order to learn. They lack the self-awareness required to recognize the need for learning strategies that more successful learners have. These students often seem disorganized and unsure about how to approach a learning task. They should be directly taught to be self-aware and to think deeply about information.

How to Teach Thinking Skills

Students need to be taught about how they think and how they can improve their learning by being aware of ways of thinking and learning. One way to do this is to teach them about the different types of knowledge. These students need to recognize that learning involves knowledge and ways of using knowledge (i.e., strategies). It is important to teach children that there are essentially three types of knowledge:

1. Content knowledge: Specific information that a person knows
2. Strategy knowledge: The way in which a person thinks or processes information
3. Metacognitive knowledge: Knowledge about how a person works with information in different ways and chooses how to process it (e.g., knowing to use a specific strategy)

Students need to understand that they learn better when they think very carefully about what they are trying to learn. They must be taught good thinking strategies for effective learning. Teachers should explicitly teach students to use a method for how to do something and think about the activity, the goal, and the desired outcome. They should also teach that a plan requires the person to

1. Think: What do I want to do? What is my goal?
2. Do: Act. Begin to complete the task.
3. Monitor: Is it working? Am I getting what I wanted?

From **Helping Children Learn: Intervention Handouts for Use in School and at Home** by Jack A. Naglieri, Ph.D., and Eric B. Pickering, Ph.D. © 2003 Paul H. Brookes Publishing Co.; 1-800-638-3775; www.brookespublishing.com

4. Modify: Do I need to modify my plan?
5. Verify: Am I finished with the task?

The teacher should teach specific strategies and carefully explain when and where they should be used. Instruction should provide a limited number of strategies, but they should be taught extensively. Emphasis is placed on reflective, not rapid, task completion that facilitates attention and concentration to the academic task. The students should be explicitly encouraged to

- Discover and use strategies
- Monitor their performance
- Generalize their use of strategies
- Be aware of the importance of strategies
- Achieve self-regulated strategy use
- Become thoughtful, planful, and evaluative

Teachers should also demonstrate good thinking skills to the students and describe good thinkers as people who are

- Patient: Understanding and ideas do not always come right away.
- Curious: Good thinkers ask questions (e.g., why, what if, when) about what they learn and look for more information.
- Focused: Good thinkers concentrate on what is being learned.
- Open: Good thinkers are receptive to other ideas and possibilities about information.
- Flexible: Good thinkers are ready to change what is learned and known to new information.
- Relaxed: Good thinkers know that they may not understand everything right away.

Who Should Be Taught Thinking Skills?

All students can benefit from discussion of good thinking skills. Students who score low in planning are particularly likely to benefit from using this instruction because it helps them gain important strategies for learning (Naglieri, 1999).

Resources

Ashman, A., & Conway, R. (1993). *Using cognitive methods in the classroom.* New York: Routledge.
Naglieri, J.A. (1999). *Essentials of CAS assessment.* New York: John Wiley & Sons.
Pressley, M., & Woloshyn, V. (1995). *Cognitive strategy instruction that really improves children's academic performance.* Cambridge, MA: Brookline Books.

From **Helping Children Learn: Intervention Handouts for Use in School and at Home** by Jack A. Naglieri, Ph.D., and Eric B. Pickering, Ph.D. © 2003 Paul H. Brookes Publishing Co.; 1-800-638-3775; www.brookespublishing.com

Strategies for Improving Organization

Being successful with schoolwork requires good organization. Successful students are thoughtful about how they organize their materials and how they plan to get their work done. Some children (especially those with attention-deficit/hyperactivity disorder) have considerable difficulty in school because they are disorganized, do not stay on task, and do not use strategies when working. These children need to be taught to use strategies and to be more organized.

Children can be explicitly taught to be more organized and to use strategies when doing school work. Educators should teach strategies in all academic areas. They should explain when and where to use strategies. Teachers should offer a few specific strategies but explain them extensively. In this approach, emphasis is placed on reflective completion, rather than fast-task completion, so that attention and concentration on the academic task is achieved. The goal is to teach strategies generated by the teacher, and later by the students, so that the students can develop and use their own strategies.

How to Teach Strategies for Organization

The teacher should provide the students with instruction about strategies for specific instructional areas (e.g., decoding, reading comprehension, vocabulary, spelling, writing, math problem solving, science).

There are two basic steps. In Step 1, teachers should tell students that 1) a plan is a method for how to do something that involves thinking about the activity and outcome and 2) a plan requires a person to

- Think: What do I want to do? What is my goal?
- Do: Act. Begin to complete the task.
- Monitor: Is it working? Am I getting what I wanted?
- Modify: Do I need to modify my plan?
- Verify: Am I finished with the task?

The second step involves explicitly encouraging students to accomplish several things when doing school work:

- Discover and use strategies
- Monitor their performance
- Generalize their use of strategies
- Be aware of the importance of strategies
- Achieve self-regulated strategy use
- Become thoughtful, planful, and evaluative

Who Should Be Taught Strategies for Organization?

Most students, especially students who are disorganized, are likely to benefit from using strategies for organization. Students who score low in simultaneous processing and planning are particularly likely to benefit from using this intervention because it helps them be aware of the need to be organized and gives them a strategic plan to help them organize (Naglieri, 1999).

Resources

Naglieri, J.A. (1999). *Essentials of CAS assessment.* New York: John Wiley & Sons.

Pressley, M., & Woloshyn, V. (1995). *Cognitive strategy instruction that really improves children's academic performance.* Cambridge, MA: Brookline Books.

From **Helping Children Learn: Intervention Handouts for Use in School and at Home** by Jack A. Naglieri, Ph.D., and Eric B. Pickering, Ph.D. © 2003 Paul H. Brookes Publishing Co.; 1-800-638-3775; www.brookespublishing.com

Improving Attention

Paying attention to the teacher and what is going on in class is very important for students. This requires that students be able to attend to specific information and resist responding to distractions in order to focus thinking. Sometimes, children need help with their attention. Some children may have a form of attention-deficit/hyperactivity disorder (ADHD), called ADHD, predominantly inattentive type (American Psychiatric Association, 1994). This handout provides help for students who struggle with attention and resistance to distraction.

Because of these problems with attending, these children may also

- Fail to complete work
- Make careless errors
- Appear easily distracted
- Not follow through on assignments, chores, and so forth
- Forget assignments, books, pencils, and other important materials

Children with attention problems may also have difficulty

- Following classroom instruction because they are not getting all the information that is provided
- Resisting distractions in the classroom
- Listening
- Working for long periods of time
- Concentrating

Students who are inattentive and have difficulties with resisting distractions need to be aware of the problem and to learn strategies for attending. Teachers and parents also need to understand that the child's behavior can be influenced by a real problem with focus of attention, and they need to develop ways to address it.

How to Help Students Improve Their Attention

Teachers and parents can do a number of things to help students improve their attention. Here are several suggestions:

- Break lessons and assignments into segments the child can complete.
- Simplify instructions and present in segments the child can manage.
- Establish a cue that the teacher or parent always uses to help the child recognize when attention is lost.
- Teach the child to systematically and carefully look at materials before responding (e.g., look at all the options before choosing an answer).

- Decrease the amount of distracting information in the environment.
- Use materials that are interesting to the child.
- Teach the child to check work using calculators, spell checkers, and other helpful items.
- Encourage children to slow down and look carefully at how words are spelled, for example.

Who Needs Help with Improving Attention?

Students who have problems attending and/or those with low scores in Attention on the CAS are likely to benefit from using this plan as a structure to help throughout the day (Naglieri, 1999).

Resources

Excellent sources for information on attention problems and other educational problems can be found at www.hood.edu/seri/serihome.html/, www.chadd.org/, and www.iss.stthomas.edu/studyguides/adhd.htm/.

American Psychiatric Association. (1994). *Diagnostic and statistical manual of mental disorders* (4th ed., text rev.). Washington, DC: Author.

Naglieri, J.A. (1999). *Essentials of CAS assessment.* New York: John Wiley & Sons.

Welton, E. (1999). How to help inattentive students find success in school: Getting the homework back from the dog. *Teaching Exceptional Children, 31,* 12–18.

Making a Plan for Organizing

Successful students organize their materials well, separating specific subjects from one another; arranging their notebooks in meaningful ways; keeping track of notes, homework, and handouts; and prioritizing the tasks they have to do. This requires that the student be planful and understand how pieces of information are related to one another and can be organized and grouped. This helps these students to be more efficient and task-oriented, which helps them study and learn successfully. The following strategies are ways to help students become more organized.

For some students, organizing material and prioritizing tasks does not come easily. They have difficulty with organization and may not see how things can be grouped together. These students often have messy, jumbled notebooks and desks. They often cannot find papers when they are requested and frequently miss assignments because they have forgotten them. Students like this may lack good organizational skills and need to be explicitly taught strategies to help them be better organized.

How to Teach Plans for Organizing

One way to help students organize their materials is by color-coding the information. For a student who has trouble keeping different subjects organized, each subject may be given a color and all materials including books, handouts, and notebook tabs should be labeled with that color. For example, for science, a student's book would be covered in orange paper, science handouts would be printed on orange paper, his or her notes would be written on orange paper, and an orange tab would be used for science in his or her notebook. Other subjects would use other colors, and a key could be made for his or her notebook listing each subject and its corresponding color. When using colored paper is not possible, colored sticky notes placed on the materials or large marks with colored markers in highly noticeable places could be used.

For a student who has trouble prioritizing material, a similar approach could be used. Instead of using colors to code different subjects, colors could be used to code for priority or urgency. A red sticky note or mark could be put at the top of homework materials, and red pencil could be used to note hot or urgent homework in a datebook. Purple could be used for less urgent work, and blue could be used for cool or least important work.

Who Should Be Taught Plans for Organization?

This strategy should be used when children need to organize and prioritize their schoolwork more efficiently. Children who are poor in planning processing are likely to need good strategies for organization and prioritizing and cannot figure out these strategies on their own (see Naglieri, 1999). Children with simultaneous processing problems might also have trouble organizing materials into meaningful groups and are also likely to benefit from learning organization strategies.

Resource

Naglieri, J.A. (1999). *Essentials of CAS assessment.* New York: John Wiley & Sons.

Summarization Strategy
for Reading Comprehension

Comprehension of written passages often demands that the child see how different parts of the story are connected. Making and understanding the connections between parts of a story and seeing the big picture requires that the child understand how all of the facts are related to one another. A reading strategy that teaches children to see how the parts of a story are connected will help them better understand the text. The technique called *summarization* is such a method. Because not all students learn how to summarize a story on their own, it is necessary to specifically teach some children how to do this.

Summarization is an effective strategy to help students enhance understanding of what is read. The method requires that a student re-write or outline only the important parts of a passage. Summarization encourages a student to look for the most important parts and determine what parts of a story are less important and what should be ignored. This also helps students see how different parts of a story relate to each other, including how parts of the text fit with the title or main topic.

How to Teach Summarization

When a student needs help, the teacher should encourage him or her to use modified or elaborated methods of summarization that best fit the student and the situation. The first step is to show the students how to summarize a story (i.e., model the strategy).

- Ask the students for the overall idea of the selected reading.
- Have the students help write a general statement about the story.
- Ask them to list the main ideas with two or three supporting ideas for each main idea.
- Give each part of the story a heading and record important details that the students help to identify.
- Ask the students what information is and is not important.
- Ask the students to describe the parts of the passage.
- Relate the important parts of the passage to the main topic and/or the title.
- Have the students write a summary that includes each of these parts.
- Have the students check the summary against what was read to see if anything important was left out.

The second step is to allow the students to practice summarization with help.

- Guide the students to underline or circle the most important parts.
- Encourage the students to look back in the text and scan (but not re-read everything).

- Encourage the use of overall or general labels for information (e.g., ducks, cows, sheep, and chickens are barnyard animals).
- Instruct the students to write down important ideas, order the ideas by importance, and ignore unimportant information.

The final step is to encourage the independent use of the summarization strategy.

- Students should independently perform the activities in Step 2.
- Have students check each other's summaries.
- Each student should check his or her own summary for key components.

After the strategy has been taught and monitored, the steps can be given to students or posted in the room as a reminder of how to use the summarization strategy. It is also important that students practice the summarization strategy and get feedback from the teacher about the quality of their summaries. Some other guidelines for teachers follow.

- Use direct explanation. Teach why, when, and where to apply summarization strategies.
- Model skills. Talk through examples and show how the skill is applied.
- Break down complicated parts into small steps.
- Summarize short paragraphs before proceeding to longer passages.
- Phase out teacher direction and phase in student use throughout instruction.

Who Should Learn Summarization?

Summarization is likely to benefit students who score low in reading comprehension. Because this intervention helps children see how the parts are all connected, it involves simultaneous processing. Students who have a simultaneous processing weakness may have a particularly difficult time reading for understanding or comprehending all the parts of a story and how they relate to each other. This technique may also be used with children who have a planning weakness. It helps them approach reading in a more strategic (i.e., planful) way that prompts them in a step-by-step manner to look for important and related parts of a story.

Resources

Two excellent resources can be found at www.tld.jcu.edu.au/netshare/learn/mindmap/ and www.iss.stthomas.edu/studyguides/mapping.htm/.

Kirby, J.R., & Williams, N.H. (1991). *Learning problems: A cognitive approach.* Toronto: Kagan & Woo Limited.
McCormick, S. (1995). *Instructing students who have literacy problems.* Upper Saddle River, NJ: Prentice Hall.
Naglieri, J.A. (1999). *Essentials of CAS assessment.* New York: John Wiley & Sons.
Pressley. M.P., & Woloshyn, V. (1995). *Cognitive strategy instruction that really improves children's academic performance* (2nd ed.). Cambridge, MA: Brookline Books.

Plans for Understanding Text

Good reading comprehension requires understanding the meaning of what is written even when it is not specifically stated. This level of reading comprehension involves relating the information the reader already knows and information from reading earlier parts of the text to information being read (Klein, 1988). *Extending questioning* and *self-questioning* are two techniques that help students make the connections among facts known, information from earlier text, and what they are currently reading so that they are better at comprehending what they read.

Extended Questioning and Self-Questioning

Extended questioning and self-questioning help students think more deeply about what they are reading and encourage them to make the necessary connections between what they know, have read, and are reading. Extended questioning is an approach to improving understanding that teaches children to analyze the text through questioning (by another person or the child him- or herself). The questions are intended to produce elaborations on the to-be-learned facts and connections to what is known.

How to Teach Extended Questioning and Self-Questioning

This can be done by individual students (through self-questioning) or students in interactive small groups (through extended questioning). This intervention can be accomplished by teaching students to ask questions about the text they have read.

1. Assign students to groups.
2. Have the students read the text.
3. Have students ask each other questions, such as:
    *   Why are you studying this passage?
    *   What are the main idea or ideas in each paragraph? Underline them.
    *   Can you think of some questions about the main idea you have underlined?
    *   What do you already know about this topic?
    *   What do you want to learn about this topic?
    *   How does this relate to what you have already learned?
    Tell students how to learn the answers to their questions by always looking back at the questions and answers to see how each question and answer provides them with more information.
4. Ask the class these questions as a group, list answers to the questions, and note the elaborations.

Who Should Learn
Extended Questioning and Self-Questioning?

This instruction is likely to benefit students who score low in reading comprehension. To comprehend text, students must understand all the parts of a text as well as other information and how it relates to the text, which requires simultaneous processing. This intervention may be helpful for students with a weakness in simultaneous processing because it helps children think more deeply about the text and how it relates to other information. This technique may also be used for children with a planning weakness. It helps them approach reading in a more strategic (i.e., planful) way that prompts them in a step-by-step manner to more deeply think about and understand what they read.

Resources

Two excellent resources can be found at www.mindtools.com/memory.html/ and www.curbet.com/speedlearn/chap2.html/.

Klein, M. (1988). *Teaching reading comprehension and vocabulary: A guide for teachers.* Upper Saddle River, NJ: Prentice Hall.
Naglieri, J.A. (1999). *Essentials of CAS assessment.* New York: John Wiley & Sons.
Pressley, M., & Woloshyn, V. (1995). *Cognitive strategy instruction that really improves children's academic performance.* Cambridge, MA: Brookline Books.

Plans for Reading Comprehension

Good readers use a variety of strategies to understand what they read. They combine their background knowledge with context cues to create meaning, they monitor their progress as they read, and they evaluate what they have read (e.g., is the content believable? does it make sense?). This thoughtful approach to reading takes good planning. Good comprehension instruction should incorporate not only decoding and understanding what is read but also approaching the text in a systematic or planful way in order to comprehend what is read. When students encounter difficult texts, they have more success if they use multiple comprehension strategies (Pressley & Woloshyn, 1995).

How to Teach Plans for Reading Comprehension

The following strategies can be easily taught and are very helpful for the reader who is struggling with comprehension, especially those who do not have good plans for comprehension. A few strategies for reading comprehension are described. Teachers should make the strategies and mental processes for good comprehension explicit in their instruction by describing how and why to use strategies. Have students engage in these activities when they read:

- Predict upcoming content by relating prior knowledge to ideas already encountered in text. This includes checking whether the predictions made were consistent with what happens in the text.
- React to text by relating ideas to prior knowledge. This is sometimes stimulated by encouraging students to integrate their background knowledge and relate it to text.
- Construct images representing the ideas in the text.
- Slow down, read more carefully, and check back in the text when the meaning is unclear.
- Generate questions in reaction to the text, perhaps by using specific questions or asking methods, with the answers then pursued by reading groups.
- Summarize the text using notes that capture the important ideas.
- Use story maps. Using this strategy is a plan to improve comprehension.

The teacher's role in strategy use includes explanation, modeling, and providing feedback. Pressley and Woloshyn (1995) suggested the following tips for teachers:

- Use strategy terms (e.g., summarizing or question generation) and define the terms when necessary.
- Model strategies by thinking aloud while applying the strategy during reading, including explaining the reasoning for applying particular strategies.
- Emphasize that strategies are coordinated with one another before, during, and after reading the text and that different strategies are appropriate at different points in a text.

- Tell students the purpose of the strategy lesson (e.g., to understand stories by using the imagery strategy along with other strategies).
- Discuss with students how they benefit from strategies use (i.e., how strategies help their comprehension), emphasizing that strategies are a means for obtaining comprehension and learning goals.

Who Should Learn Plans for Reading Comprehension?

These plans are likely to help students who have difficulty with reading comprehension. Students having difficulty in comprehension and who show deficits in planning may find the direct instruction and support of these strategies particularly helpful. Because these students may not be able to generate their own strategies for comprehension, they may find success when provided with specific and multiple strategies as well as an environment that suggests and supports strategy use.

Resources

One excellent resource can be found at www.iss.stthomas.edu/studyguides/.

Kirby, J., & Williams, N. (1991). *Learning problems: A cognitive approach.* Toronto: Kagan & Woo Limited.
Naglieri, J.A. (1999). *Essentials of CAS assessment.* New York: John Wiley & Sons.
Pressley, M., & Woloshyn, V. (1995). *Cognitive strategy instruction that really improves children's academic performance.* Cambridge, MA: Brookline Books.

Chunking for Reading/Decoding

Reading/decoding requires the student to look at the sequence of the letters in words and understand the organization of specific sounds in order. Some students have difficulty with long sequences of letters and may benefit from instruction that helps them break the word into smaller more manageable units, called *chunks*. Sometimes the order of the sounds in a word is more easily organized if the entire word is broken into these units. These chunks can be combined into units for accurate decoding. Chunking for reading/decoding is a strategy designed to do that.

How to Teach Chunking for Reading/Decoding

Teachers should first teach the children what it means to chunk or group information so that it can be remembered more easily. Use number sequences and letters for illustration (e.g., how telephone numbers are grouped). Then introduce words to be read and break the words into units, such as *re-mem-ber* for remember or *car-pet* for carpet. Try to organize the groups of letters in the word in ways that are natural (see Figure 1). For example, *re-me-mb-er* organizes the letters in groups of two, but that is not as easy to remember as *re-mem-ber* because it doesn't follow the way people naturally say the sounds.

Plan	Action
Look at the word.	"I see the word *beginning*."
Find the chunk.	"I see the chunk *ginn* in the middle."
Sound out the chunk.	"I say, 'ginn.'"
Sound out the beginning.	"I say, 'be.'"
Sound out the chunk.	"I say, 'ginn.'"
Sound out the ending.	"I say, 'ing.'"
Say the word.	"I say, 'beginning.'"

Who Should Learn Chunking for Reading/Decoding?

Children who have difficulty with sounding out words are likely to find chunking for reading/decoding helpful. Children who have difficulty working with things in order often have low successive processing ability and may find this strategy particularly helpful. This strategy also teaches children with low planning processing scores some ways of reading.

Resources

Excellent resources can be found at www.ezschool.com/, www.tld.jcu.edu.au/netshare/learn/mindmap/, and www.iss.stthomas.edu/studyguides/mapping.htm/.

Ashman, A., & Conway, R. (1993). *Using cognitive methods in the classroom.* New York: Routledge.
Naglieri, J.A. (1999). *Essentials of CAS assessment.* New York: John Wiley & Sons.

Word Families for Reading/Decoding

Reading/decoding involves making sense out of printed letters and words and includes understanding the sounds that letters represent and how letters work together to make sounds. Knowing what order letters, letter sounds, and words must be in to make sense requires careful examination of the successive series or order of the sounds. A strategy that encourages the comparison of known words to new words with similar spelling patterns may be helpful for the student having trouble with decoding a word or text for the first time. Using a strategy for decoding also provides plans needed for recognition of details such as letter orders (*ie* or *ei*), punctuation, focus on the story line, and so forth. Word families is such a strategy.

Word Families

Using word families for reading/decoding, students are taught to compare and contrast words they do not know to words they do know that are similar in order to help pronounce them. Words that sound the same often are spelled similarly, and children who know how to pronounce a word such as *tank* could make a reasonable guess at *rank*. The same student might also have a good chance at pronouncing *bank, Frank,* and *thank* if he or she were to recognize that these words are similar to *tank*. This helps the student read a word without relying on the successive nature or order of the letters in the word.

How to Teach Word Families for Reading/Decoding

One way to present this strategy is to explicitly teach it and then introduce known target words along with five to six new words that can be related to the words the students already know. Students are encouraged to learn the new words by analogy and are asked why and how the strategy helps them.

Teachers can present each word on a sheet of paper and have the students write two or three other words that share the same spelling pattern. (This also helps children with spelling problems). After this stage, the students should be asked to read passages containing the new words and to use analogies to decode them. The teacher should always model the use of analogies while reading and provide feedback for each student independently using the strategy. It is important to consider that this reading method need not be confined to simple words or comparisons, such as *bug, hug,* and *rug.* More complex words and analogies can be made; for example, the words *at, ten,* and the suffix *-tion* may be put together or analogized to form *attention.* Although not a direct combination, this analogy can serve to help the student approach the word thoughtfully and independently.

For more advanced levels of reading, the teacher should help students to automatically use the compare and contrast strategy. They may be allowed to work together, discussing how to figure out new words. Students should be encouraged to explore further words that do not match. For example, the words *pull* and *gull* look quite similar but sound different. In this stage, the teacher may begin to present words that look similar yet sound different along with the list of more difficult target words. Also, teachers may begin to explore word meanings (e.g., the words *read* and *read*), how words can be put together to form bigger words (e.g., classroom), and prefixes and suffixes. This focus on the structure of words helps children to recognize the patterns, inconsistencies, and the general make-up of words.

Once the strategy is introduced, the teacher has modeled it, and the students have practiced it, students may be simply encouraged to use the strategy whenever they encounter new words. It may be helpful for the teacher to continue to post a list of words the students know by sight that they may refer to when they encounter a new word. Throughout these stages of instruction, the teacher's role is to

- Discuss the rationale or helpfulness of the strategy
- Use and model the strategy
- Provide ample opportunity for practice and feedback
- Encourage the use of the strategy

Who Should Learn Word Families for Reading/Decoding?

Children who have poor reading/decoding skills may benefit from using word families for reading/decoding. Children who need help with successive processing skills are likely to have decoding problems (see Naglieri, 1999), and those with a planning weakness often have few plans to help them learn how to decode. This strategy for reading/decoding should be applied when the child has a successive and/or planning weakness along with reading/decoding problems.

Resources

Two excellent starting points can be found at www.iss.stthomas.edu/studyguides/ and www.hood.edu/seri/serihome.html/.

Kirby, J., & Williams, N. (1991). *Learning problems: A cognitive approach.* Toronto: Kagan & Woo Limited.
Naglieri, J.A. (1999). *Essentials of CAS assessment.* New York: John Wiley & Sons.
Pressley, M., & Woloshyn, V. (1995). *Cognitive strategy instruction that really improves children's academic performance.* Cambridge, MA: Brookline Books.

Story Grammar
for Reading Comprehension

Traditional stories that students read follow a general order. Students who are aware of this order sometimes find it easier to follow along, anticipate events, and comprehend the story. This requires an awareness of the sequential nature of stories. Instruction that makes the order of stories explicit is likely to be helpful to students. This intervention is designed to help students focus on the order of things they read. Stories generally have a specific grammar and order:

1. Introduction, including a description of
   - The main character
   - The setting
2. A problem encountered by the main character
3. Events or attempts on the part of the main character to solve the problem
4. A solution or resolution to the problem

Students who are aware of the order of a story have a structure to relate to and a way to anticipate the events of the story. Teaching this structure and anticipation reduces the amount of effort needed to read a story and helps the student focus on the important parts of the story.

How to Teach Story Grammar

A basic idea for helping a student with successive processing problems is to provide strategies to remember or practice the order of things. Instruction should begin by describing the idea of story grammar, the order of most stories, and each of the parts. Once story grammar has been described, one (or both) of two approaches can be used.

1. The student reads a story and recalls the parts and order of events in the story. This generates an opportunity for the teacher. The teacher can indicate any mistakes and instruct the student to find where he or she went wrong and try again. Simple stories should be used first; the student can proceed to more complex stories as he or she masters basic skills.
2. Students may also be provided a card (or poster on the wall) that lists the parts of a story and the order of the story. The student should be instructed to reference the card and determine where in the order he or she is.

Who Should Learn Story Grammar?

Story grammar is useful for students who have trouble following or understanding what they read. This intervention may be particularly helpful for students with successive processing problems by providing a story structure to follow (Naglieri, 1999). It is also intended to help the student focus on the order of the story.

Resources

Kirby, J.R., & Williams, N.H. (1991). *Learning problems: A cognitive approach.* Toronto: Kagan & Woo Limited.

Naglieri, J.A. (1999). *Essentials of CAS assessment.* New York: John Wiley & Sons.

Newby, R.B., Caldwell, J., & Recht, D.R. (1989). Improving the reading comprehension of children with dysphonetic and dyseidetic dyslexia using story grammar. *Journal of Learning Disabilities, 22*(6), 373–380.

Reading/Decoding Rules

For a student to decode words, he or she must make sense out of printed letters and words and translate letter sequences into sounds. This requires understanding the sounds letters represent and how they work together to make sounds. Students should know and apply a handful of useful rules for decoding words. This strategic approach to reading/decoding can help students who have difficulty with sequences.

When a child uses a rule or plan to read, the answer is obtained by thinking rather than just relying on remembering the string of letters or sounding out each letter. For example, a student may want to read the word *quiet*. The child can be taught that the letter *q* is always written with *u* and sounds like "kw." This strategy changes the task from one that demands a lot of sequencing to one that involves using a plan. The following is a number of rules and strategies for decoding (and spelling) words. These rules may be varied, and the more memorable they are for the student, the more likely they are to be used and remembered. Students need to also understand that these are rules of thumb and that the rules do not work for every word.

How to Teach Reading/Decoding Rules

It is likely to be helpful to teach a few of these rules at a time while giving the student ample opportunity to learn, use, and practice them using target words in reading and writing. Once the student has mastered using the rule correctly and has begun to recognize some of the target words on sight, new rules and words may be added. This list is not intended to be exhaustive but includes many of the major rules used for spelling. More can be found on the Internet by doing a search on spelling rules.

- The letter *q* is always written with a *u.*
- The letters *qu* always sounds like "kw."
- The letter *c* before *e, i,* or *y* sounds like "s" (e.g., *cent, city, cycle*).
- The letter *g* before *e, i,* or *y* may sound like "j" (e.g., *gentle*).
- Vowels *a, e, o,* and *u* usually sound like "ey," "ee," "ai," "oh," and "yu" at the end of a syllable (e.g., *belong, protect, futile*).
- The letters *or* may sound like "er" when *w* comes before it (e.g., *work, worm*).
- The letter combinations *ti, si,* and *ci* are used to say "sh" at the beginning of any syllable after the first one (e.g., *nation, session, special*). The combination *ch* sounds like "sh" in a word of French origin (e.g., *chic*).
- The letter combination *si* is used to say "sh" when the syllable before it ends in *s* (e.g., *session*) and when the base word has an *s* where the word changes (e.g., *tense, tension*).
- When a two-syllable word ends with a vowel and a consonant, double the final consonant when adding a vowel suffix if the accent is on the last syllable (e.g., *admit, admitted, admitting*).

- Vowels *i* and *o* may sound like "ih" and "aw" when followed by two consonants (e.g., *gift, bond*).
- The letters *dge*, which sound like "j," may be used after a single vowel that sounds like "ah," "eh," "ih," "aw," and "uh" (e.g., *badge, edge, ridge, lodge, fudge*).
- Know the *cedes* and the *ceeds.* Only one word ends in *-sede: supersede.* Only three words end in *-ceed: exceed, proceed, succeed.* All other words ending with this pronunciation use *-cede* (e.g., *concede, precede, recede*).

Who Should Learn These Rules?

Children who have trouble with basic reading and decoding may find using reading/decoding rules helpful. Also, children who score low in successive processing and who have problems with reading/decoding may find reading/decoding rules particularly helpful because they change the successive nature of reading and gives them a plan to figure out words.

Resources

Excellent resources can be found at www.ezschool.com/, www.lessonplans.com/, and www.rhlschool.com/.

McCormick, S. (1987). *Instructing students who have literacy problems.* Englewood Cliffs, NJ: Prentice Hall.
Moats, L.C. (2000). *Speech to print: Language essentials for teachers.* Baltimore: Paul H. Brookes Publishing Co.
Naglieri, J.A. (1999). *Essentials of CAS assessment.* New York: John Wiley & Sons.
Pressley, M., & Woloshyn, V. (1995). *Cognitive strategy instruction that really improves children's academic performance.* Cambridge, MA: Brookline Books.

Segmenting Words
for Reading/Decoding and Spelling

Decoding a written word requires the person to make sense out of printed letters and words and to translate letter sequences into sounds. This demands understanding the sounds that letters represent and how letters work together to make sounds. Sometimes words can be segmented into parts for easier and faster reading. The word *into* is a good example because it contains two words that a child may already know: *in* and *to*. Segmenting words can be a helpful strategy for reading as well as spelling.

How to Teach Segmenting Words

Segmenting words is an effective strategy to help students read and spell. By dividing the words into groups, students also learn about how words are constructed and how the parts are related to one another. Students should be taught that words can be broken down into segments or chunks. The teacher should present the following methods in a direct and explicit manner:

- Take the word apart. Break down the word into its component parts or syllables. For example, look at the word *reshaped*. It includes the main word *shape* with the prefix *re-* and the ending *-d*. Knowing that the main word *shape* has *re* and *d* added makes it easier to recognize than to try and sound out *r-e-s-h-a-p-e-d*.
- Identify prefixes. A *prefix* is a letter or group of letters at the beginning of a word. When a word has a prefix, imagine that there is a hyphen between the word and the prefix, and you can usually see the main word. For example, *misstep* includes the prefix *mis-* and the word *step* that are simply put together.
- Identify suffixes. Similarly, when a word has a *suffix* (i.e., a letter or group of letters at the end), you can often use a strategy similar to the prefix strategy. Just imagine a hyphen between the word and the suffix (e.g., *heart-less*).

Who Should Learn This Technique?

This instruction is likely to benefit students who are poor in reading and spelling. Because this intervention gives students strategies (i.e., plans) for solving the reading or spelling activity, it involves planning processing. For this reason, students who have difficulty with planning should be taught to use this strategy. This strategy should also be used with students who are good in planning but have a successive processing weakness and problems with reading and spelling because it will help them approach reading in a more strategic way that does not rely on their problem areas.

*From **Helping Children Learn: Intervention Handouts for Use in School and at Home** by Jack A. Naglieri, Ph.D.,
and Eric B. Pickering, Ph.D. © 2003 Paul H. Brookes Publishing Co.; 1-800-638-3775; www.brookespublishing.com*

Resources

Excellent resources can be found at www.ezschool.com/, www.lessonplans.com/, and www.rhlschool.com/.

Naglieri, J.A. (1999). *Essentials of CAS assessment.* New York: John Wiley & Sons.

Letter–Sound Awareness

English is based on an alphabet in which letters and groups of letters represent specific sounds (phonemes). A basic part of reading is recognizing that words are made up of a sequence of these sounds. This is called *phonemic awareness.* For example the letters *h, a,* and *s* include the sounds "h," "ah," and "z" and can be put together to form the word *has.* Students often sound out words they do not know using phonemic rules. To do this, they must organize the sounds of the letters in the correct sequence or order. Providing students with ways to pay attention to the sounds in words and to practice the sequencing of those sounds is likely to help them improve in reading.

How to Teach Phonemic Awareness Strategies

Phonemic awareness is not necessarily easy for students to understand because we are more concerned with the meaning of what we are saying than the sounds we make when we speak. The following strategies are ways for teachers to teach students phonemic awareness and to practice putting together words, their sounds, and the sequences of those sounds.

Here are the steps for the Letter Switch strategy:

1. Write a word on the board (e.g., *book*).
2. Guide students to sound out the word ("b-oo-k").
3. Replace or add one letter of the word on the board (e.g., *blook*).
4. Ask students to sound out the new word ("bl-oo-k").
5. Continue with variations, including changes to consonants, vowels, and beginning and ending letters.
6. Change word parts and focus on the sounds of the word parts (e.g., *booking, booked, boot, reboot*).
7. Complete each word by asking the students to use the word in a sentence. This encourages them to consider the word's pronunciation and its meaning.

Here are the steps for the Chained Words game:

1. Select 10 target words to be learned.
2. Break the words into their sound parts (e.g., "c" and "at" for *cat*), and write the parts on separate cards.
3. Place cards face down and ask the student to pick one.
4. Have the student say the word part and then pick another card.
5. Have the student say the second word part, then put it with the first, saying both word parts and blending them together.
6. Ask the student if the word is real or not. If it is not, have the student replace one card and continue with Step 4.
7. If the word is real, the student gets to keep the cards and start again. The student is finished when all the cards are gone.

As a variation, words can be longer and more cards can be picked up to make complete words. These strategies are only two of many possible ways for helping students improve their phonemic awareness. The resources section includes sources that have more instructional plans.

Who Should Learn Phonemic Awareness?

All students are likely to benefit from instruction in phonemic awareness. Organizing sequences of sounds in order to form meaningful words requires successive processing. Students who have a successive processing weakness may have a particularly difficult time with basic reading, phonemic awareness, and sounding out words. These students may find this intervention helpful.

Resources

Excellent resources can be found at www.ezschool.com/, www.tld.jcu.edu.au/netshare/learn/mindmap/, and www.iss.stthomas.edu/studyguides/mapping.htm/

Adams, M.J., Foorman, B.R., Lundberg, I., & Beeler, T. (1998). *Phonemic awareness in young children: A classroom curriculum.* Baltimore: Paul H. Brookes Publishing Co.
Moats, L.C. (2000). *Speech to print: Language essentials for teachers.* Baltimore: Paul H. Brookes Publishing Co.
Richards, R.G. (1999). *The source for dyslexia and dysgraphia.* East Moline, IL: LinguiSystems.

Plans for Word Syllables

Students must be able to break an unfamiliar word they are trying to read into its parts. This helps them sound the word out and then blend it together. For example, a child trying to pronounce the word *manipulate* can break it down into its syllables, "man-," "-ip-," "-u-," and "-late." Broken down this way, each part can be sounded out and blended together. This requires understanding the order or relationship of each letter or word part to the next. Providing students with a strategy to break words down into their syllables may prove useful.

How to Teach Syllable Division Rules

The following rules are ways for students to divide words up so they can more easily sound them out. It helps students by giving them another way to figure out a word, other than sounding each letter out.

1. Words that are made of two words, compound words, are divided between the two words (e.g., *race-car*).
2. Words with two consonants are divided between the two consonants (e.g., *lit-ter*).
3. In words with *-le*, the consonant before *-le* is include in the syllable (e.g., *cir-cle*).
4. In words that end in *-ed* after a syllable ending in *d* or *t,* the *-ed* is another syllable (e.g., *punt-ed*).
5. Words with a consonant between two vowels in which the first vowel is long are usually divided so that the consonant is with the second syllable (e.g., *pa-per*).
6. Words with a consonant between two vowels in which the first vowel is short are usually divided so that the consonant is with the first syllable (e.g., *shov-el*).
7. Words that have two different consonants between two vowels are usually divided between the consonants (e.g., *sis-ter*).

Who Should Learn Syllable Division Rules?

Students who have trouble with sounding out and reading words may find syllable division rules helpful. Students who have a successive processing weakness may have a particularly difficult time with basic reading and sounding out words, and they may find this strategy especially useful. These rules may be used to help the student to learn and practice sounding out words in a different and strategic way.

Resources

More examples, written instructions, lessons, and classroom handouts can often be found in libraries, in educational bookstores, at educational resource centers, and on-line. Excellent resources can be found at www.ezschool.com/, www.tld.jcu.edu.au/netshare/learn/mindmap/, and www.iss.stthomas.edu/studyguides/mapping.htm/.

Adams, M.J., Foorman, B.R., Lundberg, I., & Beeler, T. (1998). *Phonemic awareness in young children: A classroom curriculum.* Baltimore: Paul H. Brookes Publishing Co.
Richards, R.G. (1999). *The source for dyslexia and dysgraphia.* East Moline, IL: LinguiSystems.

Word Sorts for Improving Spelling

Spelling words correctly requires that students properly order letters. Remembering how words are correctly spelled not only requires ordering letters but also sequencing letter combinations. Children are often taught to spell through memorization of weekly spelling lists that puts much emphasis on recall of the order of the letters. Good spelling instruction should focus on the sequential features of words and the ordering of letter combinations that are associated with particular sounds. An excellent strategy for helping children become better spellers, regardless of their grade level, is a technique called *word sorts.*

Word sorts require students to organize words printed on cards or on a work sheet into groups on the basis of a particular shared spelling feature. The technique enables students to 1) generate concepts, hypotheses, and generalizations concerning the features of written words and 2) focus on the relevant aspects of how each word is spelled. In addition, word sorts help link new words to ones that are already known.

How to Teach Word Sorts

The teacher provides the students with a list of words, such as *grape, he, ape, tree, she, voice, me,* and *ice.* (The teacher may instead present the words on separate index cards.) The teacher then selects the words *grape* and *he* as categories and asks the students to sort all of the words into two columns. The students learn that sometimes the last letter is pronounced as a long *e* and other times it is silent.

Another way to sort words is to use categories that are based on shared features that the students themselves discover. This type of sort can be useful because it allows the students to figure out how the words can be grouped and how they relate to one another. It is important to have the students talk about the words while they are sorting them. This discussion may help them learn the similar ways words are spelled, see the words in groups, and promote greater understanding of how spelling works. These activities should be conducted about 10 minutes each day and can be done either with individual students or pairs of students.

Who Should Learn Word Sorts?

This instruction is likely to benefit students who are poor in spelling. Because the intervention helps children focus on the sequences of letters within groups and how groups of words with the same letters sound the same, it involves simultaneous processing. In addition, students who have not been able to learn spelling by writing or saying the sequence of letters because of poor successive processing are likely to benefit from this intervention.

Resources

Excellent resources can be found at www.sitesforteachers.com/, www.tld.jcu.edu.au/netshare/ learn/mindmap/, and www.iss.stthomas.edu/studyguides/mapping.htm/.

Kirby, J., & Williams, N., (1991). *Learning problems: A cognitive approach.* Toronto: Kagan & Woo Limited.
Naglieri, J.A. (1999). *Essentials of CAS assessment.* New York: John Wiley & Sons.
Zutell, J. (1998). Word sorting: A developmental spelling approach to word study for delayed readers. *Reading & Writing Quarterly: Overcoming Learning Difficulties, 14,* 219–238.

Chunking for Spelling

Learning to spell requires that the student remember the order of the letters that make up words. Some students have difficulty remembering the specific order of things and therefore have trouble with spelling. These children may benefit from instruction that breaks the sequence of letters into smaller, more manageable units, called *chunks.* Chunking for spelling is a specific strategy to help children do this.

Most adults can only remember about seven to nine separate pieces of information in a sequence without organizing it in a meaningful way. Information can be organized into groups to help people remember long sequences, such as a telephone number. That is why telephone numbers are organized into two groups of three numbers and one group of four. Chunking is a technique that can be used to help children (who have shorter spans of memory) remember numbers or sequences of letters for spelling.

How to Teach Chunking for Spelling

Teachers should first teach the children what it means to chunk or group information so that it can be remembered more easily. Use number sequences and letters for illustration. Then, introduce words to be learned and break the words into units (e.g., *gr-oup* for *group, re-mem-ber* for *remember*). Try to organize the groups of words in sequences that have easy-to-remember sounds. For example, *re-me-mb-er* is not as easy to remember as *re-mem-ber.*

Who Should Learn Chunking for Spelling?

Poor spellers are likely to benefit from learning chunking for spelling. Children who have difficulty remembering things in order often have low successive processing. Students who score low in simultaneous processing may find chunking particularly helpful (see Naglieri, 1999). Careful analysis of the maximum span of items that the child can remember (e.g., two or three words in order) can help determine the largest span of letters within each chunk that should be used.

Resources

Kirby, J., & Williams, N. (1991). *Learning problems: A cognitive approach.* Toronto: Kagan & Woo Limited.
Naglieri, J.A. (1999). *Essentials of CAS assessment.* New York: John Wiley & Sons.

Letter Ordering for Spelling

Spelling words and lists are a staple of the elementary classroom. Spelling of words by writing or saying the letters requires students to understand the order or sequence of the letters. Children are often challenged by learning to correctly spell new words, especially ones that cannot be spelled by sounding the word out. Good spelling instruction should focus on the successive features of words. Letter ordering is designed to help students do just that and become better spellers.

Letter ordering is a useful strategy to help develop a student's awareness of the order of sounds in words, ability to recode letters into their sounds and recognize the visual patterns in words, and ability to recall the order of the letters. This activity can be done in small groups or individually. The English language has thousands of words, and so there is an unlimited number of ways to use letter ordering.

How to Teach Letter Ordering

In letter ordering, teaching a student how to spell a word requires four steps. For each step, individual magnetic letters, letter tiles, or letters written on small pieces of paper or cardboard are used.

1. Pronounce a spelling word and ask the student to place the letter chips in the correct order.
2. After the word is formed by the student, scramble the letter chips and ask the student to say the word slowly and create it again with the chips.
3. Next, have the student say the word again and write it on a piece of paper.
4. As the child's skill increases and the complexity of the words increases, use chips to break the word into syllables or build complex words.

For difficult words, follow these steps:

1. Have the student slowly pronounce the word.
2. Ask the student to repeat the word, pronouncing the separate sounds of the word individually.
3. Tell the student to look at the word and letter chips and note how the letters match the sounds.
4. Have the student tell you which sounds go with each letter as you point to the letters in sequence.
5. Ask the student to write each letter while saying the sounds.
6. Tell the student to practice the word until he or she can write it from memory.

Who Should Learn Letter Ordering?

Students who have trouble spelling may benefit from letter ordering. Students who score low in successive processing often have difficulty with the sequencing of letters in words (see Naglieri, 1999). Also, students who have limited attention often fail to focus on the specific letters in spelling. This intervention is likely to help students who score low in successive processing, low in attention, or both.

Resources

Two excellent starting points can be found at www.iss.stthomas.edu/studyguides/ and www.hood.edu/seri/serihome.html/.

Goldstein, S., & Mather, N. (1998). *Overcoming underachieving: An action guide to helping your child succeed in school.* New York: John Wiley & Sons.
Naglieri, J.A. (1999). *Essentials of CAS assessment.* New York: John Wiley & Sons.

Mnemonics for Spelling

Spelling is an important part of education and relates to many other areas in school. Good spellers are skilled at memorizing how to correctly spell words even when the words are difficult or unpredictable. These students often have special strategies for remembering hard-to-spell words. Memorizing spelling words requires a good plan or strategy to be effective and efficient. It also requires that students understand the relationship between the letters in words. This intervention is intended to help students remember how to spell difficult words, particularly ones that are not spelled the way they sound.

Memory or mnemonic strategies are techniques for increasing learning. A *mnemonic* is a specific method that is applied to learn information. Mnemonics have been found to have considerable positive effects on student success. When students spell words and try to memorize them, they are more successful if the spelling facts are made more meaningful. Mnemonic spelling strategies make words more meaningful by combining the difficult spelling word with a part of the word in a sentence or a clever sentence or rhyme. One mnemonic uses a smaller word to focus the speller on the difficult portion of the word. Here are some examples:

- The school princi*pal* is your *pal.*
- Do not *mar* your gram*mar* with bad spelling.
- You *gain* when you bar*gain.*
- Ask someone to feed the *cat* before you leave for va*cat*ion.
- You would rather double your des*sert* than die in the hot de*sert.*
- The word *believe* has a *lie* in it.

Other mnemonics for spelling are:

- When two vowels go walking, the first does the talking.
- The silent *e* makes the vowel say its name (e.g., *tape*).
- *I* before *e* except after *c* or when sounded like "a" as in *neighbor* or *weigh.* Note that *weird* is weird, and there are a few other words that do not follow this rule (e.g., *kaleidoscope*).
- Arithmetic can be spelled using the first letter of each word in the mnemonic, "a rat in the house might eat the ice cream."
- Separate is spelled with *a rat.*

How to Teach Mnemonics

To help a student spell better using mnemonics, the teacher should first tell the student what mnemonics are and how they can help. From there, the teacher or student can identify words that are particularly difficult and create special sentences or tricks to remember them. The process of creating the mnemonic may itself help the student remember how to spell the word better.

Who Should Learn to Use Mnemonics?

Mnemonics can be helpful for all students, especially ones who have trouble remembering how to spell using traditional methods (i.e., memorization). Mnemonic strategies may be particularly helpful for students who score low in planning because they give specific strategies. It may also be helpful for students who score low in successive processing because it gives them a different way of working with the words that focuses less on the successive nature of the word (Naglieri, 1999).

Resources

Mastropieri, M.A., & Scruggs, T.E. (2000). *The inclusive classroom: Strategies for effective instruction.* Upper Saddle River, NJ: Merrill.
Naglieri, J.A. (1999). *Essentials of CAS assessment.* New York: John Wiley & Sons.

Strategies for Spelling

Spelling is an activity that requires the recall of specific letters in order and combining sounds with letter groups so that words can be recognized. Good spellers are skilled at memorizing how to correctly spell words even when the words are difficult or unpredictable. Often, spelling lists are given and students write the words over and over or rewrite them alphabetically. In order to make spelling easier for these students, give them a plan or strategy that includes various rules for spelling. A child who knows or has access to various spelling rules is likely to be able to spell many words correctly rather than just the few that have been memorized. This intervention is intended to help students use certain rules or plans to spell words, particularly ones that are commonly misspelled or are spelled in a way other than how they sound.

When a child uses a rule or plan to spell, the answer is obtained by thinking (using the plan or rule), rather than just relying on remembering the string of letters. For example, a student may want to spell *science* but may not be sure the order of the letters. If the child is taught the rule, "*i* before *e* except after *c*," then he or she is more likely to spell the word correctly. This strategy changes the task from one that demands successive processing to one that involves planning.

How to Teach Strategies for Spelling

Following are a number of rules and strategies for spelling words. This list is not intended to be exhaustive, but it includes many of the major rules used for spelling. These rules may be varied and the more memorable they are for the student, the more likely they are to be used (see the Mnemonics for Spelling handout [p. 93] for additional interventions). Students also need to understand that these are rules of thumb, and in some cases, the rules do not work for every word.

- Write *i* before *e* except after *c* (e.g., *receive, perceive, field, believe, niece, siege*).
- The letter *q* is always written with *u* and sounds like "kw."
- The vowel *y*, not *i*, is used at the end of English words (e.g., *my*).
- The majority of nouns in English form their plural by simply adding a final -*s*.
- Nouns that end with -*s*, -*z*, -*x*, -*sh*, -*ch*, and -*o* form their plural by adding -*es* (e.g., *glasses, buzzes, boxes, bushes, switches, potatoes, heroes*). Some exceptions include *studios, pianos, kangaroos, and zoos.*
- To form plurals for nouns that end in a consonant and -*y,* change -*y* to -*i* and add -*es* (e.g., *babies, spies, puppies*).
- To form plurals for nouns that end in -*f* or -*fe,* change the -*f* to -*v* and add -*es* (e.g., *shelves, wolves, knives, wives*).
- When a one-syllable word ends with one short vowel and one consonant, double the final consonant before adding a vowel suffix (e.g., *hopping, hopped*).
- When a two-syllable word ends with a vowel and a consonant and the accent is on the final syllable, double the final consonant when adding a vowel suffix (e.g., *admitted, admitting*).
- Words with a silent final *e* are written without the *e* when adding an ending that begins with a vowel (e.g., *having, writing, biking*).

- After a single vowel at the end of a one-syllable word, the *-l, -f,* and *-s* is often doubled (e.g., *full, puff, pass*).
- The letter *s* never follows the letter *x* (e.g., *boxes*).
- *All* is written with one *l* when added to another syllable (e.g., *almost, also*).
- When added to another syllable, *till* and *full* are written with one *-l* (e.g., *until, beautiful*).
- The letter *z,* never *s,* is used for the "z" sound at the beginning of a word (e.g., *zero, zipper*).
- Words beginning with a vowel and ending in *e* often lose the *e* when an ending is added or when a *y* is added (e.g., *desire/desirable, educate/education, noise/noisy*). There are some exceptions to this general rule (e.g., *likeable, lovely*).
- Only one word ends in *-sede: supersede.* Only three words end in *-ceed: exceed, proceed, succeed.* All other words ending with this sound use *-cede: concede, precede, recede.*

Some Other Strategies

- Take the word apart. Break down words into their component parts. For example, look at the word *competition.* Why is it spelled *competition* rather than *compitition*? A *competition* is a *petition* of two or more people for the same thing; they seek the same objective. You get the correct spelling by dividing the word into its two parts: *com-petition.*
- Identify prefixes. A *prefix* is a letter or group of letters at the beginning of a word. When a word has a prefix, imagine that there is a hyphen between the word and the prefix, and you can generally see the correct spelling. *Resolve* consists of *re-solve. Display* consists of *dis-play.* A word that is combined with the prefix *dis-* is spelled with *ss* if the root word begins with *s,* but only uses a single *s* if it begins with any other letter (e.g., *dissatisfy*).
- Identify suffixes. When a word has a *suffix* (i.e., a letter or group of letters at the end), you can often use a strategy similar to the prefix strategy. Imagine a hyphen between the word and the suffix, then double the letter if the word ends and the suffix begins with the same sound (e.g., *actual-ly, soul-less*). Do not double it when the two letters are different (e.g., *sincere-ly, clever-ness, heart-less*).

Who Should Learn Strategies for Spelling?

All students are likely to benefit from using strategies to help them spell. Students who have a successive processing weakness may have a particularly difficult time spelling correctly. Strategies for spelling may help students who score low in successive processing because it helps them approach spelling in a different and strategic way. Strategies for spelling may also be helpful for those who score low in planning because it gives them specific plans for spelling.

Resources

More examples, written instructions, lessons, and classroom handouts can often be found in libraries, in educational bookstores, at educational resource centers, and on-line.

Mastropieri, M.A., & Scruggs, T.E. (2000). *The inclusive classroom: Strategies for effective instruction.* Upper Saddle River, NJ: Merrill.

Story Plans for Written Composition

Writing a story requires that a student organize and write information in a way that makes sense. To do this, sentences of the story must relate to the story topic. Each sentence and paragraph of the story needs to relate to the other parts so they flow and support the main idea. Good writing instruction should focus on bringing the parts of a story together in a way that supports the main idea. Giving students procedures to follow to plan a story that is organized and fits together is likely to be helpful. A *story plan* is a diagram of the important parts of a story or text (see Figure 1). The purpose is to help the child determine the facts that might be included in the story, consider the relationships among the parts of the story, and determine how to order the information. Using story plans is an excellent method to help students write a good story.

How to Teach Story Plans

To use this intervention, follow these steps:

1. Tell the students that the story plan is a place for them to organize their thoughts.
2. Have the students fill in the parts of the story plan.

Name: _____	Date: _____
Who am I writing for?	What is the purpose of the story?
What are the facts?	
How should I organize the facts?	
In what order should I present the information?	

Figure 1. An example of a story plan form.

3. Ask the students to use arrows or draw pictures to show the connections between the various facts of their story.
4. Have the student reexamine their plan and make corrections as needed.
5. Discuss the story with the students and ask them how it was summarized in the story plan, its correctness, and its usefulness.
6. Have students write the story using the story plan.

Who Should Learn Story Plans?

This instruction is likely to benefit students who are poor in writing. Because story plans help students see how the parts of a story are related, they may be useful for students who have a weakness in simultaneous processing. Furthermore, children who score low in planning are likely to find story maps useful because they give them a way to organize or plan to write a story.

Resources

Two excellent resources related to mapping of ideas can be found at www.tld.jcu.edu.au/netshare/learn/mindmap/ and www.iss.stthomas.edu/studyguides/mapping.htm/.

Idol, L. (1987). Group story mapping: A comprehension strategy for both skilled and unskilled readers. *Journal of Learning Disabilities, 20*(4), 196–205.

Idol, L., & Croll, V.J. (1987). Story mapping training as a means of improving reading comprehension. *Learning Disability Quarterly, 10,* 214–229.

Kirby, J., & Williams, N. (1991). *Learning problems: A cognitive approach.* Toronto: Kagan & Woo Limited.

Naglieri, J.A. (1999). *Essentials of CAS assessment.* New York: John Wiley & Sons.

Pressley, M., & Woloshyn, V. (1995). *Cognitive strategy instruction that really improves children's academic performance.* Cambridge, MA: Brookline Books.

Plans for Writing

Writing paragraphs, stories, and essays is a common task for students throughout schooling and requires a lot of forethought and planning. Good writers typically generate enough content material and organize their writing to coherently convey a message. These writers create concise topic sentences and build on their topic to provide relevant information. Their sentences are logical and connected to one another. Students poor in writing often do not generate enough content and do not write sentences that relate well to one another. Furthermore, their writing is often poorly organized and does not follow a reasonable progression. Providing these students with a specific plan to follow that helps them focus on relevant information and guides them to write concise sentences that support and relate to one another is likely to be useful. This plan is a step-by-step process that teachers can use and that can be later followed by students independently. It helps students by prompting them to develop a plan for writing.

How to Teach the Plan

1. Ask students to write a sentence about something or someone using the following rules:
   - Create a sentence about which you can say something more
   - Concentrate on what the person or object does
   - Be specific about what exactly the person or object does
   - Keep the sentence short
   - Write the sentence as a statement, not a question or command
   - Have only one statement
   - Do not use a descriptive or narrative sentence

2. Have the student write three sentences about the original sentence. Sentences should be simple, clear, and direct, and they should pertain to the entire original sentence.
3. Have students write four or five sentences about each of the three sentences in Step 2. Sentences must be specific and concrete. Explain that the goal is to describe what has already been stated, *not* to introduce more information.
4. Have students insert a clear, explicit reference to the theme of the preceding paragraph in the following paragraphs.
5. Have students work to ensure that every sentence is connected with the previous sentences and makes a clear statement.

Visual displays posted in the classroom or on the students' desks can remind students of the steps and the information that should be included.

Who Should Use Plans for Writing?

Students who produce writing that is poorly structured or lacks content are likely to benefit from this plan. Students who score low in planning are also likely to benefit from using this plan because it give them a structure to help them write (Naglieri, 1999).

Resources

Two excellent resources related to mapping of ideas can be found at: www.ezschool.com/, www.tld.jcu.edu.au/netshare/learn/mindmap/, and www.iss.stthomas.edu/studyguides/mapping.htm/.

Mather, N., & Goldstein, S. (2002). *Learning disabilities and challenging behaviors: A guide to intervention and classroom management.* Baltimore: Paul H. Brookes Publishing Co.

Naglieri, J.A. (1999). *Essentials of CAS assessment.* New York: John Wiley & Sons.

Pressley, M., & Woloshyn, V. (1995). *Cognitive strategy instruction that really improves children's academic performance.* Cambridge, MA: Brookline Books.

Story Grammar for Writing

Traditionally, paragraphs, essays, and stories follow a certain order. Good writers use this order to help plan what they are going to write. This requires that students be aware of the order or sequence of what they want to write. Students who do this are likely to write in a more logical and understandable manner. This intervention is designed to help students write clearly by providing a strategy to plan the order of their writing. Creative stories often follow the order:

- Introduction
- The main character/subject
- The setting/relative factors
- Problem
- Events/circumstances
- Solution/conclusion

Students who are aware of the order of a story have a structure to follow in planning what to write. This structure provides students with a framework to write from and helps the student focus on the important parts of the story.

How to Teach Story Grammar

Instruction should begin by describing the idea of story grammar (i.e., that most stories have an order) and by describing each of the parts. Once students have a good understanding of story grammar, they can learn to use this grammar to prompt themselves about what important steps to include and in what order. The parts of a story may be posted on a wall or on the students' desks for reference.

Who Should Learn Story Grammar?

Story grammar can be helpful for all students, especially ones who have trouble writing in a logical way. This intervention is particularly useful to help students with successive processing problems and planning problems by providing a story structure to follow.

Resources

Kirby, J.R., & Williams, N.H. (1991). *Learning problems: A cognitive approach.* Toronto: Kagan & Woo Limited.

Naglieri, J.A. (1999). *Essentials of CAS assessment.* New York: John Wiley & Sons.

Newby, R.B., Caldwell, J., & Recht, D.R. (1989). Improving the reading comprehension of children with dysphonetic and dyseidetic dyslexia using story grammar. *Journal of Learning Disabilities, 22*(6), 373–380.

Teaching Vocabulary Using Visual Cues

Students are often required to learn vocabulary for a specific subject area prior to actually working in it. Science and math, for example, require that basic terminology be learned before concepts and higher-level topics can be covered. Sometimes vocabulary can be presented to a student in a way that helps comprehension. Building visual images of concepts in the words that are being taught (i.e., visual cues) is one way to do that.

Some students can learn terminology more quickly if the words they need to learn are presented in a way that is consistent with the meaning. For example, the words in Figure 1 each present a mathematical term that is drawn in a way that communicates the meaning of the word. For example, *semicircle* is presented in an arch and *slope* on an angle. This method of presentation integrates the word with the meaning in a way that is visually correct and therefore the orientation of the words communicates its meaning. This helps the student process the information in another way, which will help him or her remember it.

Who Should Learn Using Visual Cues?

All students can benefit from using visual cues, but those who are not especially good at simultaneous processing are likely to benefit from using this instruction (Naglieri, 1999) The spatial nature of the information will be helpful for these students.

Resource

Naglieri, J.A. (1999). *Essentials of CAS assessment.* New York: John Wiley & Sons.

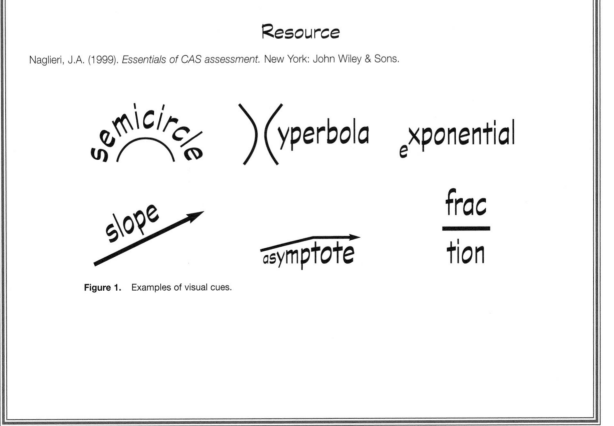

Figure 1. Examples of visual cues.

Planning by Writing Sentence Openers

Good writers start a project with a plan for what to write and how to construct the text. This requires forethought about a number of things that need to be included in what is written. Some students find it hard to write because they cannot think of what to write about or do not know what they want or need to say. It may be helpful for students to be prompted about questions that are important to answer and to use that to guide the writing process. This intervention is designed to help students use a plan for writing.

Sentence openers are idea-generating questions that help students to think of things to write. A sentence opener can be used to begin a sentence. Providing the statements or questions for students to answer acts as a cue for generating pieces of information to write about.

How to Teach Sentence Openers

When a topic is selected, students should be asked a set of questions to help them generate information to write about. Examples include

1. Describing an object
   - What does it look like?
   - What does it smell like?
   - What does it sound like?
   - What does it feel like?
   - What does it taste like?

2. Describing a sequence of events
   - What happened first?
   - What happened next?
   - What happened last?
   - Where did the events happen?
   - Who did they happen to?

3. Describing in general terms
   - Who
   - What
   - When
   - Where
   - Why
   - How

Sentence openers may be followed by other writing strategies that help the student to bring the information together in a coherent composition.

Who Should Learn Sentence Openers?

Students who have difficulty with thinking of what to write and writing with sufficient detail may find sentence openers useful. Students who score low in planning may find it difficult to begin writing because they do not have a useful way of starting the process. Sentence openers may help these students by giving them a strategy or plan to get started.

Resources

Two excellent resources related to mapping of ideas can be found at www.tld.jcu.edu.au/netshare/learn/mindmap/ and www.iss.stthomas.edu/studyguides/mapping.htm/.

Pressley, M., & Woloshyn, V. (1995). *Cognitive strategy instruction that really improves children's academic performance.* Cambridge, MA: Brookline Books.

Planning to Write

Writing successfully requires considerable planning. Successful writers include many steps in their writing, such as gathering material, organizing information, discussing their topic and ideas with others, outlining, writing, rewriting, editing, reading aloud, and so forth. Some students may not come up with or use good strategies. Often, strategies such as visualization, rehearsal through discussion, and proofing by reading aloud are not used by students. Providing students with explicit instruction in these strategies for writing is likely to help them.

Writing Strategies

Visualization: Students sometimes are unable to decide what to write. Teaching them to take time to close their eyes and imagine the topic they are going to write about, including details about who, what, when, where, why, and how, can help them get started. Visualizing themselves writing can also help the student focus.

Rehearsal: It is helpful to discuss a topic before writing. Students should be encouraged to discuss what they are going to write about before writing. Discussion of a writing topic should help the student think about what should be included and what connections should be made, especially when led by the teacher. If students are encouraged to ask questions about each other's topic, they may be clearer and more detailed in their own writing. In some cases, a student could be allowed to record his or her topic discussion or story description and then be allowed listen to it and to write it down.

Reading Aloud: Once a student is done writing, it can be very helpful if the student reads all of what has been written aloud to the teacher or to a class partner. This helps the student see the flow, logic, and clarity of what has been written and where mistakes have been made. Often students will notice mistakes themselves. This also helps the student recognize what is missing and how it can be corrected.

Who Should Learn Writing Strategies?

Students who are poor writers because they produce poorly structured content or lack of content are likely to benefit from this plan. Students who score low in planning are also likely to benefit from using this plan because it gives them the structure to help them write (Naglieri, 1999).

Resources

Excellent resources can be found at www.ezschool.com/, www.tld.jcu.edu.au/netshare/learn/mindmap/, and www.iss.stthomas.edu/studyguides/mapping.htm/.

Kirby, J.R., & Williams, N.H. (1991). *Learning problems: A cognitive approach.* Toronto: Kagan & Woo Limited.
Pressley, M., & Woloshyn, V. (1995). *Cognitive strategy instruction that really improves children's academic performance.* Cambridge, MA: Brookline Books.

Planning Facilitation for Math Calculation

Math calculation is a complex activity that involves recalling basic math facts, following procedures, working carefully, and checking one's work. Math calculation requires a careful (i.e., planful) approach to follow all of the necessary steps. Children who are good at math calculation can move on to more difficult math concepts and problem solving with greater ease than those who are having problems in this area. For children who have trouble with math calculation, a technique that helps them approach the task planfully is likely to be useful. Planning facilitation is such a technique.

Planning facilitation helps students develop useful strategies to carefully complete math problems through discussion and shared discovery. It encourages students to think about how they solve problems, rather than just think about whether their answer is correct. This helps them develop careful ways of doing math.

How to Teach Planning Facilitation

Planning facilitation is provided in three 10-minute time periods: 1) 10 minutes of math, 2) 10 minutes of discussion, and 3) 10 more minutes of math. These steps can be described in more detail:

Step 1: The teacher should provide math worksheets for the students to complete in the first 10-minute session. This gives the children exposure to the problems and ways to solve them. The teacher gives each child a worksheet and says, "Here is a math worksheet for you to do. Please try to get as many of the problems correct as you can. You will have 10 minutes." Slight variations on this instruction is okay, but do not give any additional information.

Step 2: The teacher facilitates a discussion that asks the children about how they completed the worksheet and how they will go about completing the problems in the future. Teachers should not attempt to reinforce the children. For example, if a child says, "I used xyz strategy," the teacher should not say "good, and be sure to do that next time." Instead, the teacher may probe using a statement designed to encourage the child to consider the effectiveness of the strategy ("Did that work for you?"). Discussion works best in groups in which students can learn from one another. The general goals are to encourage the children to describe how they did the worksheet. The teacher's role is to encourage the children to verbalize ideas (which facilitates planning), explain why some methods work better than others, encourage them to be self-reflective, and get them to think about what they will do the next time they do this type of work. Here are a list of suggested probes:

- "How did you do the page?"
- "Tell me how you did these problems."
- "What do you notice about how this page was completed?"
- "What is a good way to do these pages, and what did this teach you?"
- "Why did you do it that way? What did you expect to happen?"

- "How are you going to complete the page next time so you get more correct answers?"
- "What seemed to work well for you before, and what will you do next time?
- "What are some reasons why people make mistakes on problems like these?"
- "You say these are hard. Can you think of any ways to make them easier?"
- "There are many problems here. Can you figure out a way to do more?"
- "Do think you will do anything differently next time?"

Step 3: The teacher gives each child a math worksheet and says, "Here is another math worksheet for you to do. Please try to get as many of the problems correct as you can. You have 10 minutes."

Aids to Facilitate Discussion

- Make an overhead of a blank worksheet so the children can see it during discussion.
- Make an overhead of a completed worksheet (with the name omitted).
- Have the children do a blank worksheet as a group on the overhead projector.

It is important for teachers not to say things like, "Watch me. This is how to do it," "That's right. Good, now you're getting it!" "You made a mistake. Fix it now," or "Remember to use your favorite strategy." This discourages discussion among the students and does not help to meet the goals of the strategy.

Who Should Learn Planning Facilitation?

This instruction is likely to benefit students who are poor at mathematics calculation. Because planning facilitation helps students focus on their approach to solving problems, it helps them be more careful or planful. Children who score low in planning are likely to improve the most from this instruction.

Resources

Good starting points for mathematics intervention can be found at www.mathgoodies.com/, www.sitesforteachers.com/, and www.mathprojects.com/.

Kirby, J., & Williams, N. (1991). *Learning problems: A cognitive approach.* Toronto: Kagan & Woo Limited.
Naglieri, J.A. (1999). *Essentials of CAS assessment.* New York: John Wiley & Sons.
Naglieri, J.A., & Johnson, D. (2000). Effectiveness of a cognitive strategy intervention to improve math calculation based on the PASS theory. *Journal of Learning Disabilities, 33,* 591–597.
Naglieri, J.A., & Gottling, S.H. (1997). Mathematics instruction and PASS cognitive processes: An intervention study. *Journal of Learning Disabilities, 30,* 513–520.
Pressley, M., & Woloshyn, V. (1995). *Cognitive strategy instruction that really improves children's academic performance.* Cambridge, MA: Brookline Books.

Number Squares for Math Concepts

Math concepts and skills (e.g., counting, counting by twos and threes, counting by odd and even numbers) require the student to work with numbers in a specific order. Children often rely on rote memory techniques to remember how to count. Some children need to be taught the relationships among the numbers directly and in a way that helps them understand how the numbers relate to one another. Using number squares is a good strategy to help students understand and see the relationship between numbers.

Number squares can help students learn the conceptual relationships between numbers by helping them see the patterns in numbers and how certain numbers relate to others in a graphic way. Number squares give a particular order or seeable pattern to an otherwise abstract and nonvisual concept. This can give greater meaning, understanding, and enjoyment in learning mathematics.

A number square is a large square divided into 100 smaller squares, 10 by 10. Each small square is numbered, 1 to 100, starting at the upper left square as shown in Figure 1. Having 10 numbers in each row focuses the student's attention on the basic groupings of numbers in base 10. A student can explore the grid and see how numbers relate to each other (e.g., how the numbers in each row down have the same second digit and how the numbers in each column across have the same first digit).

In the case of teaching a concept such as odd and even numbers, the student can be encouraged to explore the grid and shade in every other number. Doing this exposes the student not only to the meaning of odd and even numbers but also to how they look and relate to one another. The student can see that every number is either odd or even and that a class of numbers is odd or even (1, 11, 21, 31, 41, and so on in the ones column). If even numbers are the focus, the grid can serve as a guide or prompt for counting by twos. Furthermore, this same grid can be used to teach multiplication. Take the case of multiplying by 6. A student can be instructed to use a new grid, count by 6 and shade each sixth number (see Figure 2). Then, when a fact is presented, say 6 multiplied by 8, the student can count up eight shaded blocks and arrive at the answer. This allows the student to see the answer and the pattern involved in it. Number squares can be used in many ways:

- As a way to present a new concept (e.g., counting, odd or even numbers, number groups, multiplication)
- As an exploration device (e.g., "What patterns do you see?")
- As a tool for the student to refer to like a calculator

How to Teach Number Squares

A teacher instructing adding, counting, or multiplying by fours may wish to provide students with a number square and ask them to shade every fourth number, starting from number 1 (see Figure 3). The teacher may then ask questions about the pattern created, how the numbers are the same or different in each row and column, and how it can help solve problems. The teacher then may encourage the students to have this shaded square handy so that they can refer to it when presented with a number problem. A new square can be provided for each new number or fact.

1	2	3	4	5	6	7	8	9	10
11	12	13	14	15	16	17	18	19	20
21	22	23	24	25	26	27	28	29	30
31	32	33	34	35	36	37	38	39	40
41	42	43	44	45	46	47	48	49	50
51	52	53	54	55	56	57	58	59	60
61	62	63	64	65	66	67	68	69	70
71	72	73	74	75	76	77	78	79	80
81	82	83	84	85	86	87	88	89	90
91	92	93	94	95	96	97	98	99	100

Figure 1. A standard number square.

1	2	3	4	5	6	7	8	9	10
11	12	13	14	15	16	17	18	19	20
21	22	23	24	25	26	27	28	29	30
31	32	33	34	35	36	37	38	39	40
41	42	43	44	45	46	47	48	49	50
51	52	53	54	55	56	57	58	59	60
61	62	63	64	65	66	67	68	69	70
71	72	73	74	75	76	77	78	79	80
81	82	83	84	85	86	87	88	89	90
91	92	93	94	95	96	97	98	99	100

Figure 2. A number square that shows counting by sixes.

1	2	3	4	5	6	7	8	9	10
11	12	13	14	15	16	17	18	19	20
21	22	23	24	25	26	27	28	29	30
31	32	33	34	35	36	37	38	39	40
41	42	43	44	45	46	47	48	49	50
51	52	53	54	55	56	57	58	59	60
61	62	63	64	65	66	67	68	69	70
71	72	73	74	75	76	77	78	79	80
81	82	83	84	85	86	87	88	89	90
91	92	93	94	95	96	97	98	99	100

Figure 3. A number square that shows counting by fours.

From there, the students may be encouraged to use number squares on their own to approach new concepts and problems.

Who Should Learn Number Squares?

Number squares can be used in many areas of math and at many different age levels. It gives the student a way to look at the patterns formed by a sequence of numbers. This changes the task from one that demands considerable successive processing to one that requires simultaneous processing. The creation of patterns makes a sort of visible rhythm that can be better remembered by the student. Therefore, this strategy appears especially useful for children who have trouble with number concepts and may be particularly useful for students who score low in successive processing.

Resources

Two excellent starting points for both students and teachers are available at forum.swarthmore.edu/dr.math/dr-math.html/ and www.mathgoodies.com/.

Kirby, J.R., & Williams, N.H. (1991). *Learning problems: A cognitive approach.* Toronto: Kagan & Woo Limited.
Naglieri, J.A. (1999). *Essentials of CAS assessment.* New York: John Wiley & Sons.
Orton, A. (Ed.) (1999). *Pattern in the teaching and learning of mathematics.* New York: Cassell.
Pressley, M.P., & Woloshyn, V. (1995). *Cognitive strategy instruction that really improves children's academic performance.* Cambridge, MA: Brookline Books.

Plans for Basic Math Facts

Learning basic addition, subtraction, multiplication, and division facts typically demands that the student memorize a large amount of information. Students who memorize math facts learn the information in order. For example, students are often encouraged to say or write the basic facts in sequence (7 + 8 = 15). Writing or saying this sequence of numbers puts the task into a linear order with at least five steps. A strategy that teaches children to obtain the correct answer without relying on memorization of a string of digits can be helpful. Because many students may not use strategies to learn their basic facts, they should be specifically taught to do so.

Plans to Learn Basic Math Facts

Using plans to learn math facts is an effective strategy because the answer is obtained by thinking (using the plan or method) rather than by relying on remembering the string of numbers. The method requires that the student use some rule or method of arriving at the answer. For example, the "doubles plus one" rule can be used to help students find the answer to 7 + 8 without relying on memory of the answer because the answer can be obtained by thinking as follows: "7 + 8 . . . well, 7 + 7 is 14, so 7 + 8 has to be one more than 14, so the answer is 15." Here are some strategies for addition:

- 2 + 2 is a car with four wheels.
- 3 + 3 is the legs of an ant.
- 4 + 4 is an octopus with four legs on each side.
- 5 + 5 is fingers on both hands.
- 6 + 6 is an egg carton (or the legs of two ants).
- 7 + 7 is two weeks.
- 8 + 8 is two spiders.
- 9 + 9 is two baseball teams.

Here are some rules for multiplication:

- 0 multiplied by any number is always 0 ($0 \times 9 = 0$)
- 1 multiplied by any number is always that number ($1 \times 7 = 7$)
- 2 multiplied by a number will end in a zero or an even number ($2 \times 2 = 4$, $2 \times 10 = 20$)
- 5 multiplied by any number gives an answer that must end in 0 or 5. 5 multiplied by any number involves counting by fives, as when telling time from a standard clock. 5 multiplied by an even number is half that number with a 0 added ($5 \times 4 = 20$, $5 \times 8 = 40$)
- 9 multiplied by any number can be solved by a plan: take one away from the multiplier. That number goes into the tens place. Subtract that number from 9. That number goes into the ones place, which gives the answer ($9 \times 8 = 72$, $8 - 1 = 7$, which goes in the tens place. $9 - 7 = 2$, which goes in the ones place for a final answer of 72). 9 multiplied by any number is that number multiplied by 10 minus the number ($9 \times 7 = 63$. $10 \times 7 = 70$, and $70 - 7 = 63$). Of course, the 10s rule should be mastered before this one.

- The answer to 10 multiplied by any number always ends in 0. Simply put a 0 on the end of the multiplier (4 × 10 = 40)

After learning all of the multiplication rules, only the following facts must be specifically memorized: 3 × 3; 3 × 4; 3 × 6; 3 × 7; 3 × 8; 4 × 4; 4 × 7; 4 × 8; 6 × 7; 7 × 7; 7 × 8; 8 × 8. Teachers should teach a few rules at a time, allowing students to learn each one thoroughly before moving to the next. After the rules have been taught and monitored, they can be posted in the room for independent use. Throughout instruction the teacher should

- Use direct explanation. Teach why, when, and where to use these rules.
- Model skills. Talk through examples, and show how the skill is applied.
- Provide practice with feedback
- Phase out teacher direction and phase in student use throughout instruction

Who Should Learn Plans for Math Facts?

This instruction is likely benefit students who have had problems learning math facts. Because this intervention encourages children to solve the problems by applying a strategy, it involves a lot of planning. If a child scores low poor in successive processing, he or she is likely have problems memorizing math facts because they are presented in a specific order. Students with successive processing problems should be taught to use these math strategies or plans. This technique may be used to help students approach multiplication and division in a strategic way that does not rely on their problem area (successive processing).

Resources

Two excellent starting points for both students and teachers are available at forum.swarthmore.edu/dr.math/dr-math.html/ and www.mathgoodies.com/.

Goldstein, S., & Mather, N. (1998). *Overcoming underachieving: An action guide to helping your child succeed in school.* New York: John Wiley & Sons.
Muschla, J.A., & Muschla, R.G. (1995). *The math teacher's book of lists.* Upper Saddle River, NJ: Prentice Hall.
Naglieri, J.A. (1999). *Essentials of CAS assessment.* New York: John Wiley & Sons.

Cuisenaire Rods and Math

Children regularly must work with numbers and understand the abstract meanings and relationships the numbers have. Understanding the relationships between the numbers or their specific order is sometimes difficult for students. Often, students rely on techniques such as rote memory to remember how to count, calculate, and recall basic facts. When a child attempts to learn these facts by rote (e.g., counting by evens: 2, 4, 6, 8, 10), the numbers remain abstract. Using a strategy that helps students relate to numbers in a graphic way can be helpful for many students. Using Cuisenaire rods is a good strategy to do this.

Cuisenaire rods are a set of carefully designed rods in graduated length and color that use color to identify length. For example, a red rod represents a unit of 2 and it is twice as long as a white rod, which represents a unit of 1. This helps children identify each rod and its relationship to others. With number values assigned to the rods, children can see number relationships from patterns the rods create. Cuisenaire rods can help a student see the patterns involved in numbers and how they relate to others in a graphic way. This can give the student greater meaning, understanding, and enjoyment in the learning of mathematics.

How to Teach Using Cuisenaire Rods

Cuisenaire rods can be used in many ways and at different grade levels. They can be used to introduce and work with numbers, simple addition, subtraction, multiplication, division, and other number concepts, such as fractions. The key to using cuisenaire rods for teaching mathematics is to encourage students to see the physical relationships the rods have to each other. Doing this helps students recognize the concepts of larger, smaller, the same, sums, differences, products, factors, and fractions.

Who Should Learn to Use Cuisenaire Rods?

Children who have trouble understanding numbers and mathematics are likely to benefit from using Cuisenaire rods. Because successive processing is involved when a child works with numbers in order, students who are weak in successive processing may find Cuisenaire rods particularly helpful. For a child who is weak in successive processing, this method encourages the student to use a different way of thinking about and working with the numbers—for example, how the numbers can be related to shapes or patterns and grouped together visually. Cuisenaire rods can help a student see the patterns involved in numbers and how certain numbers relate to others in a graphic way. They give a particular physical representation or pattern to otherwise abstract and nonvisual concepts.

Resources

More examples, written instructions, lessons, and classroom handouts can be found on-line at www.etacuisenaire.com. A few web pages with information and lessons are www.xlrn.ucsb.edu/

~jhurley/classes/micros/lesson_plans/Qrods1.html/, www.iit.edu/~smile/ma9208.html/, and www.crpc.rice.edu/CRPC/GirlTECH/silha/Lessons/cuisen2.html/.

Davidson, P.S. (2002). *Idea book: Mathematics activities for Cuisenaire Rods at the primary level.* Vernon Hills, IL: ETA/Cuisenaire.

Kirby, J.R., & Williams, N.H. (1991). *Learning problems: A cognitive approach.* Toronto: Kagan & Woo Limited.

Naglieri, J.A. (1999). *Essentials of CAS assessment.* New York: John Wiley & Sons.

Orton, A. (Ed.) (1999). *Pattern in the teaching and learning of mathematics.* New York: Cassell.

Pressley, M.P., & Woloshyn, V. (1995). *Cognitive strategy instruction that really improves children's academic performance.* Cambridge, MA: Brookline Books.

TouchMath for Calculation

Young students are asked to perform many types of counting, addition, subtraction, multiplication, and division problems throughout the school day. Performing mathematics requires understanding and using numbers in sequence. When students find counting and performing equations in their head difficult, they often use their fingers to count. This is a helpful strategy in that it makes the task more concrete so they can feel the order of the numbers. However, this strategy may be inefficient and may not lend itself to the written completion of math problems. TouchMath is another strategy for calculation that helps children see a pattern in an otherwise abstract and nonvisual concept.

How to Teach Using TouchMath

TouchMath is a multisensory method of computation that may be used in all four processes of addition, subtraction, multiplication, and division. It begins with counting the correct number of touchpoints corresponding to the number value placed on the face of each numeral. Figure 1 is used to help children learn to conceptualize by touching and counting. This creates a visual representation of the number that illustrates the number value, eliminates guesswork, and reduces errors. Teachers should follow these guide-lines to use TouchMath.

- Provide students with a sheet of TouchMath numbers.
- Teach TouchMath points: each number has dots that are to be touched and counted in a specific order. Single touchpoints are touched and counted one time. Double touchpoints are touched and counted twice.
- Model counting and using correct touching and counting patterns on numerals 1–9.
- Provide worksheet problems with TouchMath numbers.
- Have students practice using the strategy several times so that they may master it.

Phasing Out TouchMath

- Once children master the use of touchpoints with guidance, they may be instructed that the touchpoints can be used even when they aren't actually on the number.
- Provide guided practice without actual touch points.
- After the skill is mastered, phase out the touch points.

Figure 1. An example of TouchMath numbers. (*Key:* ● *single point,* ○ *double point,* ⬤ *triple point*). (From Bullock, J. [2002]. *TouchMath: The Touchpoint Approach for Teaching Basic Math Computation* [4th ed.]. Innovative Learning Concepts, 6760 Corporate Drive, Colorado Springs, CO 80919-1999; 800-888-9191. Reprinted with permission.)

Who Should Learn TouchMath?

TouchMath should be used for children who have problems with addition, subtraction, multiplication, and division. It may be particularly useful for students who score low in successive processing (see Naglieri, 1999). It may be especially helpful for the child who scores low in successive processing and scores high in the area of simultaneous processing because the strategy helps the child to see numbers and how number values relate to others in a physical way.

Resources

More information can be found by calling 1-800-888-9191 and on-line at www.touchmath.com. A web search on TouchMath also provides a vast source of information, suggestions, lessons, and examples.

Bullock, J. (2002). *TouchMath: The TouchPoint approach for teaching basic math computation* (4th ed.). Colorado Springs, CO: Innovative Learning Concepts.

Kirby, J.R., & Williams, N.H. (1991). *Learning problems: A cognitive approach.* Toronto: Kagan & Woo Limited.

Naglieri, J.A. (1999). *Essentials of CAS assessment.* New York: John Wiley & Sons.

Orton, A. (Ed.) (1999). *Pattern in the teaching and learning of mathematics.* New York: Cassell.

Pressley, M.P., & Woloshyn, V. (1995). *Cognitive strategy instruction that really improves children's academic performance.* Cambridge, MA: Brookline Books.

Part–Whole Strategy for Math Calculation

Math calculation is a complex activity that involves recalling of basic math facts, remembering procedures to be followed, working carefully, and checking one's work. Children who are good at math calculation can move on to more difficult math concepts and problem solving with greater ease than those who are having problems in this area. A strategy that teaches children to planfully and carefully work with math problems is likely to help. The part–whole strategy is such a method.

Researchers have found that children can be taught to perform better when doing math calculations if they are taught to solve the problems carefully. The method called *part–whole strategy* (Van Luit & Naglieri, 1999) teaches children to break down math problems into more manageable parts. This method is also easy to apply and helps students approach problem solving in a planful way.

How to Use Part–Whole Strategy

Part–whole strategy should be directly taught to students who are learning basic math calculation. Students should be taught to use this strategy in a flexible way and to think aloud as they do the math. The teacher should lead the discussion of the strategy, encourage strategies developed by the students, and assist children to reflect about the value of the methods they have suggested. Teachers should explicitly teach strategies that help students see that calculation problems can be broken into parts and solved more easily. The following strategies should be taught:

1. *Addition of parts:* An addition problem, such as 10 + 9, can be broken into parts: 5 + 5 + 9
2. *Doubling:* A problem like 8 × 6 can be broken into two parts; 4 × 6 and 4 × 6, which when added yields the same answer as 8 × 6
3. *Doubles plus 1:* When doing simple addition such as 7 + 8, break the problem into two like numbers (7 + 7), then add 1 (7 + 7 + 1 = 15)
4. *Doubles plus 2:* A problem such as 7 + 9 can be solved by adding 1 to the smaller number and subtracting one from the larger number (7 + 1 = 8) + (9 − 1 = 8) so 8 plus 8 is 16.
5. *Reconstruction:* A problem such as 7 + 9 can be modified into a simpler form: 10 + 7 − 1 = 16. Similarly, a multiplication problem like 9 x 5 can be modified to (10 × 5) − 5. Also using this strategy, 9 × 8 = (10 × 8) − 8 = 72.
6. *Multiplication as addition:* Multiplication is repeated addition, so 6 × 4 is the same as (6 × 1) + (6 × 1) + (6 × 1) + (6 × 1).

Who Should Learn Part–Whole Strategy?

The part–whole strategy should be used when children need to learn math calculation. It may be particularly helpful for students who are poor in planning or successive processing. Children who are poor in planning processing (see Naglieri, 1999) are unlikely to have good strategies for doing math calculation and will not figure out these strategies on their own. Children with successive processing problems have trouble remembering basic facts when they are taught in a sequence ($9 \times 8 = 72$).

Resources

Two excellent starting points for both students and teachers are available at forum.swarthmore. edu/dr.math/dr-math.html/ and www.mathgoodies.com/.

Naglieri, J.A. (1999). *Essentials of CAS assessment.* New York; John Wiley & Sons.

Naglieri, J.A., & Johnson, D. (2000). Effectiveness of a cognitive strategy intervention to improve math calculation based on the PASS theory. *Journal of Learning Disabilities, 33,* 591–597.

Pressley, M., & Woloshyn, V. (1995). *Cognitive strategy instruction that really improves children's academic performance.* Cambridge, MA: Brookline Books.

Van Luit, J.E.H., & Naglieri, J.A. (1999). Effectiveness of the MASTER strategy training program for teaching special children multiplication and division. *Journal of Learning Disabilities, 32,* 98–107.

From **Helping Children Learn: Intervention Handouts for Use in School and at Home** by Jack A. Naglieri, Ph.D., and Eric B. Pickering, Ph.D. © 2003 Paul H. Brookes Publishing Co.; 1-800-638-3775; www.brookespublishing.com

Seven-Step Strategy
for Math Word Problems

Math word problems are often difficult for many children. Word problems are much easier when a student knows and uses effective strategies to solve them. Students who approach math word problems without a strategy often make procedural and computational errors. Interventions for math word problems should target both basic skills and use of strategies "to enable students to be thoughtful problem solvers" (Scheid, 1993, p. 9). In addition, academic instruction must be tailored to the cognitive needs of individual students. Giving students some strategies or plans for doing word problems can be very helpful to them.

A Plan for Working on Math Word Problems

Math word problems especially require a careful and systematic approach, a plan that includes developing ways to do the problem as well as checking that the solution is reasonable and correct. Strategy use, or good planning, is critical for coming up with an effective way of approaching the problem and monitoring the effectiveness of the strategy. Children who have poor planning skills will find these problems especially hard to solve, and therefore they should be instructed to use a plan.

How to Teach the Plan for Doing Word Problems

Following are the basic steps for teaching plans for doing word problems.

1. Read (for understanding and getting information)
   - Read the problem. If you do not understand, read it again.
   - Ask, "Have I read and understood the problem?"
   - Check for understanding as you read the problem

2. Paraphrase (use your own words to restate the problem)
   - Underline the important information. Put the problem in your own words.
   - Ask, "Have I found the important facts? What is the question I looking for?"
   - Check that the information goes with the question

3. Visualize (a picture or a diagram of the problem)
   - Make a drawing or a diagram.
   - Ask, "Does the picture fit the problem?"
   - Check that the information goes with the question

4. Hypothesize (make a plan to solve the problem)
   - Decide how many steps and operations are needed. Write the symbols (+, −, ×, /).

- Ask, "If I do it this way, what will I get? If I do this, then what do I need to do next? How many steps are needed?"
- Check that the plan makes sense

5. Estimate (predict the answer)
   - Round the numbers, do the problem, and write the estimate.
   - Ask, "Did I round up and down? Did I write the estimate?"
   - Check that you used the important information

6. Compute (do the arithmetic)
   - Do the operations in the right order.
   - Ask, "How does my answer compare with my estimate? Does my answer make sense? Are the decimals or money signs in the right places?"
   - Check that all the operations were done in the right order

7. Check (make sure everything is right)
   - Check the computation.
   - Ask, "Have I checked every step and calculation, and is my answer right?"
   - Check that everything is right. If not, go back. Then, ask for help if you need it.

Who Should Learn the Plan for Word Problems?

All students are likely to find using this plan helpful for doing word problems. Math word problems involve all the PASS processes. Successive processing is involved when a child has to remember the ordering of relevant information. Attention is involved when the child must separate relevant from irrelevant details in the word problem. Simultaneous processing is very important so that the child can see how all the information in the problem is related. However, students who score low in planning are likely to benefit from using this plan as a structure to help them work through math word problems (Naglieri, 1999).

Resources

Two excellent starting points for both students and teachers are available at: forum.swarthmore.edu/dr.math/dr-math.html/ and www.mathgoodies.com/.

Montague, M. (1992). The effects of cognitive and metacognitive strategy instruction on mathematical problem solving of middle-school students with learning disabilities. *Journal of Learning Disabilities, 25,* 230–248.

Montague, M. (1995). Cognitive instruction and mathematics: Implications for students with learning disorders. *Focus on Learning Problems in Mathematics, 17,* 39–49.

Montague, M. (1997). Cognitive strategy instruction in mathematics for students with learning disabilities. *Journal of Learning Disabilities, 30,* 164–177.

Montague, M., Applegate, B., & Marquard, K. (1993). Cognitive strategy instruction and mathematical problem-solving performance of students with learning disabilities. *Learning Disabilities Research & Practice, 8,* 223–232.

Montague, M., & Bos, C. (1986). The effect of cognitive strategy training on verbal math problem solving performance of learning disabled adolescents. *Journal of Learning Disabilities, 19,* 26–33.

Naglieri, J.A. (1999). *Essentials of CAS assessment.* New York: John Wiley & Sons.

Scheid, K. (1993). *Helping students become strategic learners.* Cambridge, MA: Brookline Books.

Chunking Strategy for Multiplication

Multiplication is a task that involves recalling of basic math facts, remembering procedures to be followed, working carefully, and checking one's work. Sometimes, children need a way to organize the numbers when doing multiplication, especially when they try to do the work by breaking the multiplication problem into parts. Providing these students with a strategy to do basic multiplication facts can help them be more successful.

The multiplication strategy of chunking helps children break the numerical problem into separate parts that can be more easily solved. Children who have trouble doing multiplication may benefit from this strategy because it helps them break the problem down in more manageable parts. The way the strategy works is that the child is taught to break the numbers into groups (i.e., chunks) that can be more easily managed. For example, 2×8 is the same as counting by twos eight times. If a child is taught to use a slash mark (/) for each step of counting by twos, when the eighth slash mark is written the problem is solved. Use the steps to teach the chunking strategy.

1. Read the problem: $2 \times 8 = $ _____
2. Point to a number you know how to count by twos
3. Make the number of slash marks indicated by the other number (in this case the number 8).
4. Count by twos as you touch each mark: "2, 4, 6, 8. . ."
5. Stop counting at the last mark: ". . .,10, 12, 14, 16"
6. The number you stopped on is the answer: "16"

Who Should Learn
the Chunking Strategy for Multiplication?

This strategy can be useful for students having difficulty learning multiplication facts. It can also be very useful for students who are poor in planning or successive processing. Children who score low in planning processing are unlikely to have good strategies for doing multiplication and will not figure out these strategies on their own (see Naglieri, 1999). Children with successive processing problems have trouble remembering basic facts when they are taught in a sequence ($9 \times 8 = 72$). These children are also most likely to benefit from learning calculation strategies.

Resources

Two excellent starting points for both students and teachers are available at forum.swarthmore.edu/dr.math/dr-math.html/ and www.mathgoodies.com/.

Naglieri, J.A. (1999). *Essentials of CAS assessment.* New York: John Wiley & Sons.

Naglieri, J.A., & Johnson, D. (2000). Effectiveness of a cognitive strategy intervention to improve math calculation based on the PASS theory. *Journal of Learning Disabilities, 33,* 591–597.

Pressley, M., & Woloshyn, V. (1995). *Cognitive strategy instruction that really improves children's academic performance.* Cambridge, MA: Brookline Books.

Shapiro, E.S. (1989). *Academic skills problems direct assessment and intervention.* New York: The Guilford Press.

Van Luit, J.E.H., & Naglieri, J.A. (1999). Effectiveness of the MASTER strategy training program for teaching special children multiplication and division. *Journal of Learning Disabilities, 32,* 98–107.

Crossed Lines Multiplication Strategy

Multiplication is a skill that involves remembering basic math facts. Students can learn these facts in a variety of ways. Some children write the facts over and over, others might refer to a multiplication matrix that is posted in the room or kept at the students' desks so that it can be referred to for help. These methods help students commit facts to memory. Sometimes students cannot immediately remember facts and need a strategy to figure out the correct answer on their own. Doing this can also help them remember the facts better. The following strategy is a specific plan students can use to figure out math facts and help them arrive at the correct answer.

Crossed Lines Multiplication Strategy

Students can use the crossed lines multiplication strategy to figure out a multiplication fact that has not been committed to memory. It is a strategy not unlike counting on your fingers, that makes the abstract concept of multiplication more concrete. This makes it easier for students to work with and understand.

How to Teach Crossed Lines Multiplication Strategy

This strategy can be easily taught. Here is an example using the steps for this strategy.

1. Ask, "What is 3 times 2?"
2. Draw lines across for the first number in the problem (3).
3. Draw lines down for the second number in the problem (2).
4. Count the number of times the lines cross to get the answer to the problem.
5. For future facts, including either of the two numbers already used, additional lines can be added (e.g., 3×3).

Who Should Learn
the Crossed Lines Multiplication Strategy?

This strategy should be used when children need to learn multiplication. Children who score low in planning processing are unlikely to have good strategies for doing multiplication and will not figure out these strategies on their own. Children with successive processing problems have trouble remembering basic facts when they are taught in a sequence ($9 \times 8 = 72$). For this reason, students who are poor in planning or successive processing may find this strategy particularly useful.

Resources

Naglieri, J.A. (1999). *Essentials of CAS assessment.* New York: John Wiley & Sons.

Naglieri, J.A., & Johnson, D. (2000). Effectiveness of a cognitive strategy intervention to improve math calculation based on the PASS theory. *Journal of Learning Disabilities, 33,* 591–597.

Pressley, M., & Woloshyn, V. (1995). *Cognitive strategy instruction that really improves children's academic performance.* Cambridge, MA: Brookline Books.

Shapiro, E.S. (1989). *Academic skills problems direct assessment and intervention.* New York: The Guilford Press.

Van Luit, J.E.H., & Naglieri, J.A. (1999). Effectiveness of the MASTER strategy training program for teaching special children multiplication and division. *Journal of Learning Disabilities, 32,* 98–107.

More Strategies for Math Word Problems

Math word problems are among the most challenging activities for children and adults. Being able to do them is an important skill to have because we often have to figure out math-related problems in everyday life. Word problems involve many skills, concepts, and procedures. In order to manage all of these demands, children should use systematic strategies that will aid in the successful completion of the problem. The strategies should include consideration of the basic skills needed to solve the problem, the procedures required, and the methods needed for success. Here are some basic strategies for math word problems:

1. Read the problem slowly and carefully.
2. Cross out information that is not relevant.
3. Draw a diagram of the problem or visualize it.
4. State the facts and the problem in your own words.
5. Estimate what the answer should be.
6. Calculate the answer and check against the estimate.
7. Check your work.
8. Remember you have to know the basic math facts to get the correct answer.
9. Be persistent.
10. Be sure you read the problem correctly.

Students should be taught how to classify arithmetic word problems into four types: change, combine, compare, and equalize.

1. Change: These problems involve values that are changed as the result of some action by the student. For example, Jack had two pencils. Mary gave him three more. How many pencils does Jack have now? Students should be taught to think about how to represent this type of problem. For example, the student can visualize Mary handing Jack her three pencils to put with his two.
2. Combine: Word problems of this type require the child to use a more general view of the mathematical situation by computing a total based on a new way of organizing the problem. Jack has two pencils. Mary has three pencils. How many pencils do they have altogether? By asking this question, a new concept of the two children as a group is required.
3. Compare: In these problems, the quantity of the sets does not change, but the operations demand that a relative relationship be determined. For example, Jack has two pencils. Mary has three pencils. How many more pencils does Mary have than Jack? Children should be taught to recognize the greater than/less than nature of this type of problem and that it will typically involve subtraction.
4. Equalize: These problems require that the values in the problem be equalized. For example, Jack has two pencils. Mary has three pencils. How many more pencils

does Jack need in order to have as many as Mary? Children should be taught to recognize equalize problems and expect that it will likely involve both subtraction and addition.

Who Should Learn a Plan for Word Problems?

All students are likely to find using this plan helpful for doing word problems. Math word problems involve all the PASS processes. Successive processing is involved when a child has to remember the ordering of relevant information. Attention is involved when the child must separate relevant from irrelevant details in the word problem. Simultaneous processing is very important so the child can see how all the information in the problem is related. However, students who score low in planning (Naglieri, 1999) are likely to benefit from using this plan as a structure to help them work through math word problems.

Resources

Two excellent starting points for both students and teachers are available at forum.swarthmore. edu/dr.math/dr-math.html/ and www.mathgoodies.com/.

Geary, D.G. (1999). *Children's mathematical development.* Washington, DC: American Psychological Association.

General Strategies for Test Taking

Doing well on a test not only requires the student to know specific information, it also requires that the student be good at test taking. Students who prepare for a particular test, have an idea or plan for what to study, and think about how to answer the questions are likely to do well on a variety of tests. Some students need to be taught good test preparation and test-taking strategies to be successful. Teaching general test-taking strategies can help students be planful and strategic in their approach to answering questions during a test. Although some students use strategies when they take tests, others do not and need to be explicitly taught good test-taking skills.

How to Teach General Strategies

First, students should be taught that specific strategies for test taking can be helpful. They should be told how they can prepare and to take tests in strategic ways. To accomplish this goal, children should be taught several steps.

1. Prepare for the test by asking,
    * *What is the content of the test?* In order to be prepared, students need to find out exactly what the content of the test will be. Students should also consider what *will not* be on the test. Asking about specific materials they should study can also be helpful.
    * *What is the test format?* Will the questions on the test be multiple choice, fill in the blank, multiple choice, or essay? How specific will the questions be? When studying, students should think of questions and answers in the format of the test. Their teachers can help by giving practice tests.

2. Take the test carefully and be relaxed.
    * Be careful. Students should be prompted to take a test very carefully and not to rush. Breaking a test session down into two parts may be helpful. Using this strategy, students use the first half of the test session to take the test and the second half to check their work. This can assist in curbing students who want to rush to finish without checking.
    * Relax. Specifically instruct students to relax before taking a test. Give them time to do so. Consider having students stretch, breathe deeply, and even close their eyes and daydream before a test. Teacher comments can also be very important in helping students relax.

Who Should Learn
General Strategies for Test Taking?

Most students can benefit from these strategies. Students who score low in planning could find these strategies particularly helpful because these students may have trouble developing test-taking strategies on their own. These strategies may also be helpful for students who are particularly anxious about taking tests.

Resource

Scruggs, T.E., & Mastropieri, M.A. (1992). *Teaching test-taking skills: Helping students show what they know.* Cambridge, MA: Brookline Books.

Strategies for
Multiple Choice, Matching, and True–False Tests

Careful preparation and planning is necessary for good performance on multiple choice, matching, and true–false tests. Students can be more successful if they plan and study for the specific kind of test they are taking. There are many different strategies for doing multiple choice, matching, and true–false tests. Multiple choice, matching, and true-false tests require the recognition of specific facts. These tests can be especially tricky, and, therefore, students need to be aware that they can use specific strategies for these tests. Although some students use strategies when they take the test, others do not and need to be explicitly taught good test-taking skills.

How to Teach Test Taking for Objective Tests

Specifically teach students to

- Think of what the answer might be before reading the answer choices
- Carefully and completely read the questions
- Highlight key words in the question
- Eliminate answers that are clearly incorrect
- Draw a picture to help organize the question
- Estimate an answer to eliminate options that are likely wrong
- Read ALL the answer choices, even the ones that look wrong
- Read the question and answers twice
- Not pick the longest answer
- Not choose an answer based on the location (first, middle, last)

Who Should Learn Strategies
for Multiple Choice, Matching, and True–False Tests?

Most students can benefit from these strategies. Students who score low in planning could find the strategies particularly helpful because these students may have trouble developing test-taking strategies on their own. These suggestions may also be helpful for students who are particularly anxious about taking tests.

Resource

Scruggs, T.E., & Mastropieri, M.A. (1992). *Teaching test-taking skills: Helping students show what they know.* Cambridge, MA: Brookline Books.

Strategies for Written Tests

Written tests are particularly difficult for students because they require students to know the information that is being asked and students have to answer in a coherent and logical way. These types of tests require considerable preparation and specific strategies for completing the assignment. Using a good strategy for taking written exams can help students be successful because they can work more efficiently and therefore produce a better answer. Although some students use strategies when they take tests, others do not and need to be explicitly taught good test-taking skills.

How to Teach Strategies for Written Tests

Students should be specifically told how they can take written tests using strategies that will help them produce a better response. Scruggs and Mastropieri (1992) suggested that students be taught to use the acronym SNOW for essay test taking: *S*tudy the question; *N*ote important points; *O*rganize the information; and *W*rite directly to the point of the question. Students should be taught to

1. Study the question carefully
2. Be sure to completely answer the question that is asked
3. Make a list of the specific points
4. Do not leave a question unanswered
5. Provide an answer even when they are not sure because partial credit is better than no credit
6. Use words and ideas from the question
7. Check their work when they are finished

Who Should Learn Strategies for Written Tests?

Most students can benefit from these strategies. Students who score low in planning could find the strategies particularly helpful because these students may have trouble developing test-taking strategies on their own. These suggestions may also be helpful for students who are particularly anxious about taking tests.

Resource

Scruggs, T.E., & Mastropieri, M.A. (1992). *Teaching test-taking skills: Helping students show what they know.* Cambridge, MA: Brookline Books.